THE BODHRÁN

THE
BODHRÁN

Experimentation, Innovation,
and the Traditional Irish Frame Drum

COLIN F. HARTE

CHARLES K. WOLFE MUSIC SERIES
Ted Olson, Series Editor

The University of Tennessee Press
Knoxville

The Charles K. Wolfe Music Series was launched in honor of the late Charles K. Wolfe (1943–2006), whose
pioneering work in the study of American vernacular music brought a deepened understanding of a wide range
of American music to a worldwide audience. In recognition of Dr. Wolfe's approach to music scholarship,
the series will include books that investigate genres of folk and popular music as broadly as possible.

LIBRARY OF CONGRESS CATALOGING-IN-PUBLICATION DATA

Names: Harte, Colin F., 1981– author.
Title: The bodhrán: experimentation, innovation, and the traditional Irish frame drum / Colin F. Harte.
Description: [First.] | Knoxville: The University of Tennessee Press, 2020. | Series:
The Charles K. Wolfe music series | Includes bibliographical references and index. | Summary:
"Colin F. Harte traces the bodhrán from its early origins in Irish traditional music to its present-day
resurgence in Irish American folk music. Harte includes chapters on the instrument's historical
and organological development, experimentation and innovation in playing styles over time,
and a study of the instrument's performative practices. The central academic focus of the text is the recent,
rapid developments in bodhrán design, performance practices, and teaching the bodhrán
to a new generation of musicians" — Provided by publisher.
Identifiers: LCCN 2020004175 (print) | LCCN 2020004176 (ebook) |
ISBN 9781621905554 (paperback) | ISBN 9781621905561 (adobe pdf)
Subjects: LCSH: Bodhrán — History. | Bodhrán — Performance — Ireland.
Classification: LCC ML1038.B63 H37 2020 (print) | LCC ML1038.B63 (ebook) | DDC 786.9/519 — dc23
LC record available at https://lccn.loc.gov/2020004175
LC ebook record available at https://lccn.loc.gov/2020004176

Contents

Illustrations

Acknowledgments

I would like to thank my loving family for their support, time, and effort. Much love and thanks to my mother, Liam, Aidan, and Rory. In loving memory of my aunt Claire. Many thanks to the numerous bodhrán makers, players, educators, enthusiasts, and scholars who were so generous with their time and knowledge, without whom this book would not be possible.

Foreword

Few "accidental" discoverers of this book — people who happen upon it on-line or in a catalog, bookstore, or library — would have been able to identify the instrument pictured on the book's cover before seeing its name on the cover in all its Gaelic glory. Aficionados of Irish music, however, are quite familiar with the instrument, and they will no doubt welcome this opportunity to immerse themselves in its deep and enchanting history.

The subject of this book is the Irish frame drum known as the bodhrán (bow-rän), a word translatable as "deafening," which alludes to the instrument's sometimes booming timbre. Providing the pulse-beat to traditional Irish music for at least a century (1920s recordings document bodhrán players accompanying various instrumentalists), the bodhrán has historically been overshadowed in Irish music ensembles by such melodically felicitous instruments as uilleann pipes, fiddles, flutes, and accordions. By not taking for granted the bodhrán's signature contributions to the Irish music soundscape — rhythms ranging from hypnotic to propulsive — this book casts a long-overdue spotlight on an instrument which originated ages ago as a winnowing sieve used to separate grain from chaff.

According to ethnomusicologist and this book's author Colin Harte, the bodhrán largely took its modern form in the early-twentieth century after enterprising musicians converted it from a sieve into a percussion instrument. A round hollow wooden frame bearing a stretched-out animal skin, the bodhrán could be readily built by hand, and thus it remained a folk instrument for decades. The creation of the Irish Free State in 1922 inspired certain builders to produce versions of the instrument — inscribed with the insignia "Souvenir of Ireland" — to sell to tourists. This was an early acknowledgment of the iconic role of the bodhrán in embodying and symbolizing the Irish people's ingenuity and resourcefulness.

Harte's book traces the instrument's evolution from the Bronze Age to the forefront of Irish musical consciousness during the Irish music revival of the 1960s and beyond, with the bodhrán showcased in such leading revivalist groups as The Chieftains (as performed by Peadar Mercier and Kevin Conneff), Planxty (Christy Moore), and the Irish-Scottish band the Boys of the Lough (Robin Morton). Through various techniques practiced by the different masters of the instrument, the bodhrán could either rumble or roar, alternately hypnotizing listeners by infusing a tragic ballad with a heartbeat, or energizing dancers by establishing the brisk tempo needed to guide moving feet. The book addresses the various techniques for playing the instrument: a player can strike the skin top with the whole hand, with individual fingers, or with a hardwood stick alternately referred to as a tipper, beater, or, in Gaelic, cipîn; and a player can dampen the sound of the bodhrán by placing the palm against the drum skin.

Replete with approximately forty images visually illustrating the cosmos of the bodhrán — its major players, its material components, and its stylistic techniques — Harte's book offers a lucid introduction to and the first sustained scholarly exploration of an instrument which has long been an integral part of Irish music's artistic and cultural identity.

TED OLSON
East Tennessee State University

THE BODHRÁN

Introduction

As a number of musicians quietly collect themselves, moving their chairs into a circle, a bit of conversation begins to bubble in a lively pub. These musicians have gathered to perform Irish traditional music in an informal context known as a session. The resident leader of the session is an accordionist seated next to a fiddler, flautist, and guitarist. The last musician to arrive is a man holding a circular bag containing a bodhrán and several tippers. After a brief greeting, the music commences. Reels and jigs are organized into sets rapidly following one another interspersed with snippets of conversation pertaining to local politics, new recordings, humorous stories, and personal anecdotes. The accordionist, fiddler, and flautist provide the melodic content, the guitarist offers harmonic and rhythmic accompaniment, and the bodhrán player offers percussive rhythmic accompaniment. The pub patrons continue eating and drinking. Occasionally a heated musical moment captures their attention only to be shortly redirected back to their conversation. This musical context is familiar to Irish traditional musicians and enthusiasts alike and serves as one of the most common performance contexts for the bodhrán.

Unlike any other instrument associated with Irish traditional music, the bodhrán in the last fifty years has been significantly altered in design, performance techniques, and music contextual practices. The bodhrán is the Irish circular frame drum, which has experienced a rapid period of development and expansion spurred on by professionalization, bodhrán maker innovation, performer creativity, acoustic analysis, and organological experimentation. In part, this text tries to make sense of the myriad changes in organology (the study of musical instruments), performative practices, pedagogy, and repertory. It also examines the historical development of the bodhrán including an analysis of the changing role and function of the instrument in Irish traditional music and culture. Drawing from a host of interviews over several years in Europe and North America, this work provides a voice for multiple perspectives regarding the bodhrán. Participants include bodhrán makers, professional performers, educators, amateur musicians, historians, and enthusiasts. Growing out of rich ethnographic interviews, this text serves as the definitive reference for understanding and navigating the developments in the bodhrán's history, organology, performance practices, and repertory.

The bodhrán is the focus of this ethnography because it has changed from a maligned, peripheral Irish traditional instrument to a recognizable, versatile percussion instrument used in various musical traditions and contexts. This period of change provides a fascinating window into larger tectonic shifts that have occurred within Irish traditional music as a result of professionalization, cosmopolitanism, and globalization.

Despite a number of introductory pedagogical texts, the bodhrán has not been fully explored in an ethnographic sense. My research methodology was based on participant observation, interviews, video and audio documentation, musical involvement, written correspondence, and archival research. I participated in musical contexts ranging from formal class lessons and rehearsals to informal house performances, sessions, and concerts with local musicians in North America and Europe. By employing a comprehensive fieldwork methodology that engages communities on different fronts, I was able to gain a detailed understanding of the bodhrán's role in these communities. Multisession interviews with key informants (educators, makers, community members, performers, Irish traditional musicians, and enthusiasts) represented a wide spectrum of instrumental expectations and perspectives. These interviews along with other musical activities were documented through audio and video recordings.

The research sites varied considerably based on venue, region, and country, although most field visits were conducted in Ireland and the northeastern United States. It should also be noted that the bulk of interviews occurred in Ireland, Scotland, England, the United States, and Canada. During my research, I used compact, portable digital equipment for data collection and processing for recording music events and interviews. Since many visits included classroom observations, discrete compact digital equipment was essential in order to minimize any in-class distractions.

The audio and video recordings facilitated my interviews and analyses of bodhrán making, performance, and instruction. The photographs document the makers, performers, teachers, and students interviewed, types of instruments, performance spaces, and types of rehearsals and performances.

Over the course of seven years, I accumulated a sizeable number of field interviews, notes, and participatory experiences. Inspired by research participants' generosity of time and information, it was evident that an ethnography explaining the instrument's unique and often misunderstood history, evolving musical role, and variations in design, usage, and pedagogy filled a gap in Irish traditional music scholarship.

Due to the global spread of the bodhrán and sudden increase in interest and popularity, the participants are from locations around the globe. Therefore, communication depended on all possible forms: in-person meetings, letters, email, telephone, Skype, instant messaging, texting, and online forums. Through these interviews, idiosyncratic approaches to bodhrán making, performance, and pedagogy emerged whose collective variations pushed the instrument into new realms of artistic and instrumental expressions.

Based on the analysis of bodhrán historical texts, ethnographic interviews, and instrument observations, I constructed a historical narrative of the organological development of the bodhrán and its associated performative practices. Chapter 1 provides a historical basis for discussing current trends in bodhrán design, performance, and pedagogy. This historical foundation grounds the reader in the possible origins of the bodhrán, its musical roles in various cultural practices, and the techniques involved in building older models. Seminal bodhrán makers and performers are discussed in detail, analyzing their influential contributions in chronological order.

Chapter 2 examines recent experiments and innovations in bodhrán design, and specific models are analyzed. Leading makers are discussed in relation to their motivations for bodhrán construction, scientific experiments, composite materials, drum design, and technological innovations. The impact of new performative practices and Irish traditional music is examined at length. An analysis of the impact of the professionalization of Irish traditional music and, subsequently, bodhrán making is included. In addition, a further elaboration upon the impact of the commercialization and standardization of bodhrán production serves to explain recent progress in bodhrán making.

Chapter 3 explores a variety of innovative and idiosyncratic performative practices as executed by a host of performers. Each facet of bodhrán performance is analyzed including sticking, pitch control, skin manipulation, rhythmic patterns, the mapping of rhythms on the drum head, different percussive conceptualizations of the bodhrán, microphone placement, technological experimentation, and computer software. I also discuss the impact of professionalization upon bodhrán performance. The recent expansion of bodhrán performative contexts and diverse musical roles is studied and explained in relation to the concepts of cosmopolitanism, globalization, and imagined communities. This chapter focuses on the different sonic and performative possibilities of the bodhrán as realized by competent performers.

In conjunction with advances in bodhrán design and performative practices, chapter 4 discusses the repertory of the bodhrán. An analysis of different bodhrán sources is detailed extensively. A review of the multitude of academic publications, scores, instructional materials, film and television, literary fiction, online resources, and seminal recordings are provided.

One
HISTORY OF THE BODHRÁN

Irish traditional music includes instrumental music (tunes) and vocal music (songs). Tunes take different musical forms such as the jig (6/8 meter), reel (4/4), slip jig (9/8), hornpipe (4/4), polka (2/4), barn dances (4/4), marches (4/4, 6/8), slides (12/8), waltzes (3/4), and slow airs. These tunes can be performed as individual pieces or strung together as medleys. Irish instrumental music was originally played to accompany dances and thus features lively, rhythmic playing.

The tradition's primacy of melody ensures that performers must memorize and master a vast repertoire of tunes. Melodic instruments such as the harp, uilleann pipes, fiddle, tin whistle, flute, accordion, and concertina have historically been at the center of Irish traditional music. Peripheral accompaniment instruments such as the guitar, piano, bouzouki, bodhrán (Irish frame drum), and bones have more recently been incorporated into instrumental performances. Among the tradition's instrumental hierarchy, the melodic instruments retain a top tier due to their historic involvement in the music genre as well as their ability to perform the tune repertoire. Accompaniment instruments are placed in a secondary tier, since they do not provide the central melodic content. Their musical accompaniment is viewed as supplemental and not essential to the tune-based music form. The single melodic line of the tune is highly prized in performance settings where accompanists are encouraged to follow the melodic line as closely as possible. This musical aesthetic is germane to percussion accompaniment as well, resulting in performances that closely imitate the melody.

The secondary status of the bodhrán has yielded a plethora of jokes. Seamus Ennis quipped that the drum was best played with a pen knife.

Other jokes hover around the uselessness of the drum and player such as the bodhrán player who left his drum in an unlocked car only to return to find three more drums left in the backseat. Of course, lighthearted humor is part of the camaraderie of playing Irish traditional music. If the tone of the conversation becomes sour or angry, there's no expectation for a bodhrán to tolerate it. One solution to this problem according to Rónán Ó Snodaigh is simply to "give them a good belt." However, the best antidote for animosity toward the bodhrán player is to exemplify good musicianship, keen listening, and sound judgment.

The popularity of Irish traditional music has waxed and waned in Ireland, Europe, and North America. The tradition enjoyed an artistic renaissance during the folk revival of the 1960s and a resurgence of interest in the 1990s after the international success of *Riverdance*. This led to a diversification of performance contexts (concerts halls, pub sessions, local dances, music clubs, and private homes). The banjo, guitar, bouzouki, bodhrán, and bones became incorporated with greater frequency.

Bodhrán player at a session. (*An Beal Bocht*, Colin Harte, September 9, 2018.)

Sessions are typically informal opportunities where amateur and professional musicians perform. Repertoire and arrangements are spontaneously selected by attending musicians. Within this performance context, there are frequently one or more melodic players with the possibility for one harmonic accompanist (e.g., guitar, bouzouki) and one percussive accompanist (e.g., bodhrán). Sessions are typically organized and run by accomplished melodic players who influence tune selection and session etiquette. As tunes are performed, the bodhrán player is expected to provide unobtrusive, rhythmic accompaniment. It is within this milieu that the bodhrán player has shaped and refined his musical role.

A session can be a complex environment to maneuver as a bodhrán player. The drummer must provide rhythmic accompaniment while adjusting drum pitches in the bass register. Often complementing the rhythmic and harmonic accompaniment of a guitarist, the drummer must also closely follow the melody. In addition, he must maneuver through the matrix of session musician hierarchy. With tasteful accompaniment and social bonds, a bodhrán player can participate in sessions. However, the drummer oblivious to these social nuances and assumed aesthetic expectations will find short shrift with the larger musical community. As a pub patron in Limerick, Ireland, I saw a local resident buying a novice bodhrán player a pint of Guinness with the caveat that he could only consume it if he promised to stop playing for the night. These subtle and sometimes rude exchanges can easily be avoided through skilled musicianship and good social judgment.

THE HISTORY OF THE BODHRÁN

In order to fully understand modern bodhrán playing and its development, it is essential to trace the organological history of the instrument. A historical overview of significant developments regarding its design and performance practices is outlined here in order to illuminate some innovations and experiments. Specific organological changes, performance practices, key actors, and pedagogy will be discussed in later chapters.

The specific origins of the bodhrán are the subject of debate and suffer from a lack of instrumental evidence due to the natural decay of organic materials (wooden frame and animal skin) that were used to create frame drums. The frame drum is a percussion instrument consisting of one or two membranes stretched over an open circular frame. Due to the simple frame design of the bodhrán, it shares organological commonalities with various frame drums such as the *doira* of Afghanistan (Vallely 1999, 28), the *tar, riq,* and *bendir* from the Middle East and North Africa, and the *tamorra* and *tamburello* from Southern Europe (Forsthoff and Kruspe 2013, 21).

Based on these similarities, several migratory hypotheses concerning the origin of the bodhrán in Ireland have circulated.[1] Scott Morrison posits that the Celts brought the frame drum to Ireland after encountering it during their westward movement through Europe (1500 BC to 60 AD) (Morrison 2011, 38). Ríonach uí Ógáin argues that the bodhrán can be traced back to the Bronze Age in Ireland as evidenced by the use of winnowing sieves to separate the cereal grain from the chaff. These sieve artifacts are labeled as sieves, skin drums, and tambourines by the National Museum of Ireland (Ógáin 2002, 141–42).

A second hypothesis suggests that the frame drum may have been carried by the Romans to the British Isles during the first century BC. Roman mosaics depict musicians being accompanied by a small frame drum. A third hypothesis claims that the Vikings could have brought fish skin or reindeer skin oval frame drums from Lapland, Finland, during their conquest of Ireland from 800 AD through 1014 (Such 1985, 10). These hypotheses are not supported by conclusive evidence and thus remain speculative and intriguing.

Sligo musician and historian Seamus Tansey mythologizes the origins of the bodhrán. During an interview with me in 2015, he explained:

> In the old times, the bodhrán was a religious instrument. It was used on certain occasions. The certain occasions were midsummer's eve [summer solstice] bonfire night. That was June 23, when the sun was the highest in the sky, and they used to have bonfires celebrating that. It was pagan. Then at Christmas time, the day after Christmas Day, December 26, was the old winter solstice. It was wren's boy day. The sun, they believed in the old times, died in the sky at that time. In the days coming up to what we call Christmas, they beat the bodhráns to bring it alive in the sky. And when St. Stephen's Day came and they saw the sun coming, they thought the sun came alive with the beating of their drums. Now if you notice, the bodhrán is in a circle just like the sun. It is in the form of the sun. And it was left up for the rest of the year until midsummer's eve. When the bonfires were there, they brought out the bodhráns and beat the bodhráns with the music and dancing to celebrate the rebirth of the sun. When the Christians came, they put the Christian and pagan together with the rebirth of the sun and the birth of the son of God.

THE DOMESTIC ORIGINS OF THE BODHRÁN

In regard to the domestic origins of the bodhrán in Ireland, scholars speculate that the bodhrán was created from a round sieve or winnow used in rural farming. The sieve was commonly used in Ireland up to the 1930s and was called a *wecht* (lowland Scotland and England), *wicht* (Ireland), *dallán* (Ireland), *dollan* (Isle of Man), and *croder-croghen* (Cornwall, England).[2] The *dallán* was made by stretching an animal skin over a branch that was cut along its length.[3] The skins of goats, calves, deer, donkeys, horses, greyhounds, and rabbits were used (McCrickard 1987, 1). They were treated in various ways including covering the skin with lime, burying it in the ground for nine days or more, removing the clay, scraping off the hair and remaining fat, and then tightly stretching it to a frame (Ógáin 2002, 142). The round shape was held through bark strips lashed around the outside. The wet skin was then placed around the edges and pushed inward to dry firmly on the rim. The process of attaching the skin to the frame without tacks was known as lapping (McCrickard 1987, 2). During farming, the *dallán* was held by this rim. The *dallán's* design would have made for a natural, convenient instrument whose sheepskin could produce a percussive sound (Hannigan 1991, 68).

Similarly, the parallels between frame drums and grain sieves or skin trays exist beyond the realm of the bodhrán. The dual purpose of early frame drums as percussive instruments and grain sieves or skin trays appear to be as old as the instrument itself. This notion is supported by the common name for both types of artifacts. In ancient Sumer of southern Mesopotamia (one of the earliest, documented urban civilizations of mankind dating from ca. 3500 BC), the noun *adapa* (*adapu*) was used to describe both a grain measure

Wecht. (St Fagans National Museum of History, Colin Harte, August 15, 2017.)

and a square frame drum, while in medieval North Africa the noun *ghirbāl* had a dual meaning referring to both a sieve and a round frame drum. In the Iberian Peninsula, we find that at least in Aragon during the fourteenth century a skin tray or similar utensil was also known by the name *pandero*. Therefore, there exists a long-standing precedent of the dual usage of the skin sieve as an agrarian tool and a musical instrument.

In the *Topographia Hibernica* written in 1185, Welsh Norman royal clerk Gerald of Wales noted that the Irish delighted in the music of the harp and tympanum (frame drum or tambourine), while the Scottish used the harp, tympanum, and crowd (bowed lyre). Although the frame drum is not named as a bodhrán, the observation of the existence of a frame drum in Ireland by a traveling foreign chronicler does exist (O'Meara 1982, 94). In the fifteenth century, *Rosa Anglica* references the bodhrán in relation to *tympanitis*. This medical text notes that one symptom that occurs is that the stomach resounds when struck like a timpan or bodhrán (Ó Bharáin 2008a, 52). This early reference to the bodhrán as a percussion instrument (the exact nature of the drum's construction is still unknown) indicates a possibly lengthy existence in Ireland.

Sir John Halkett of Pitfirrane Bart (1720–1793), His Wife and Family. (David Allan. Courtesy of the National Galleries of Scotland.)

The Penny Wedding. (James Stewart; after Sir David Wilkie.
Courtesy of the National Galleries of Scotland.)

A frame drum resembling the bodhrán is depicted in an oil painting entitled *Sir John Halkett of Pitfirrane, 4th Bart (1720–1793), Mary Hamilton, Lady Halkett, and Their Family,* by David Allan in 1781. The Scottish patrons are shown amid a lively musical performance featuring a frame drum with inset jingles being played by hand alongside a lute and dancers. *The Penny Wedding* by Alexander Carse in 1819 depicts a gregarious Scottish wedding reception with a frame drum hanging upon the right wall. These paintings are exhibited at the National Galleries Scotland. Both demonstrate the existence and use of frame drums that resemble bodhráns in Scotland. One can speculate that, due to the continuous exchanges between Scotland and Ireland, frame drums were present and used in Ireland in the late eighteenth century and early nineteenth century as well.

The bodhrán is also featured in *Snapp-Apple Night* by Daniel Maclise (1833), exhibited at the Royal Academy London. The painting displays a festive house party, hosted by Father Mathew Horgan of Co. Cork, filled with merriment, the consumption of food and drink, and dancing accompanied by a small group of musicians featuring a bodhrán being played with a stick

Snapp-Apple Night. (Courtesy of The Elisha Whittelsey Collection.)

A Shebeen Near Listowel. (Courtesy of the TRIARC-Crookshank-Glin Collection.)

and the opposite hand held behind the skin. A watercolor painting attributed to Bridget Maris Fitzgerald entitled *A Shebeen near Listowel* (ca. 1842) shows a bodhrán with jingles inserted into the frame being played with the hand.

The word *booraan* appears in Jacob Pool's unpublished glossary of non-standard English words that were commonly found in the dialect of south Wexford that he collected during the late eighteenth and early nineteenth century. Pool defines *booraan* as a drum, tambourine, or sieve for winnowing corn (Ó Bharáin 2008, 52). The word later appears in 1904 in an Irish-English dictionary compiled by Patrick S. Dineen, defined as a wooden, sievelike device with a sheepskin bottom. In 1935 the word bodhrán similarly appears in Mc Cionnaith's English-Irish dictionary, which indicates that the word was commonly used in Connaught and Ulster dialects.

EARLY BODHRÁN RECORDINGS OF THE 1920S AND 1930S

A number of Irish traditional music 78 rpm recordings from the 1920s, stemming from the emerging recording industry in New York and to a lesser degree in Chicago, also appeared in Ireland and provide evidence of bodhrán accompaniment. The flute player Tom Morrison (1889–1958) from Co. Galway released five recordings made in New York, which feature John Reynolds playing bodhrán.[4] Reynolds's playing demonstrates an open, ringing tone whose sticking closely follows the tune (Morrison and Reynolds 1927: Columbia 33210-F). In 1928 a recording of the "Connaught Reel" displays Reynolds's dampened bodhrán playing, which can be attributed to his own partial muting on the back of the skin with his hand as well as his distance from the recording microphone. The result is that an open ringing tone is absent from the recording, and instead a dampened sound that emphasizes the stick attack on the skin is present (Columbia 33293-F). Another 78 rpm recording featuring Tom Morrison, John Reynolds, and pianist Ed Gagen captures Reynolds playing a bodhrán with jingles that he shakes at the end of eight-bar phrases (Columbia 33247-F). Reynolds's bodhrán playing demonstrates a keen understanding of the rhythmic structure and phrasing of the tunes and provides lively, supportive percussive accompaniment.

THE WREN BOYS PROCESSION

Prior to the 1950s, the bodhrán featured prominently in processional rituals and harvest festivals, such as St. Stephen's Day on December 26, May Day on May 1, and St. Brigid's Day on February 1 (O'Mahoney 1999, 34). As documented by folklorist and photographer Caoimhín Ó Danachair (Irish

Folklore Commission, 1935–71) in 1946 in Co. Limerick, the bodhrán was used as part of the wren boys processional ritual occurring on St. Stephen's Day (Lysaght 2002, 261).[5] The bodhráns featured in Ó Danachair's photographs are of varying sizes, some with several jingles in the frame and a visible double-ended tipper. The wren boys, disguised in costumes and often with darkened faces, would go from house to house performing selected music on portable instruments (e.g., tin whistle, flute, concertina, fiddle, bodhrán) to willing village hosts where they would receive a small compensation for later potation. The St. Stephen's Day ritual also involved hunting and burying a wren (Ó Súilleabháin 1974, 5).

This processional ritual had its roots in ancient Celtic and Christian lore. Therefore, it was common to hear the bodhrán being played for such festive occasions.[6] Birds, particularly ravens and wrens, were viewed as liminal intermediaries capable of crossing between realms (sky-earth, earth-spirit world) and possessing divine powers. The Druids used the flights of these birds as auguries. Old Irish linguists speculate that the Gaelic word for wren, *dreoilín*, is a conflation of two Gaelic words, *draoi éan*, or Druid bird (Duffy "The Wren").

1947 Wren Boys procession in Athea, Co. Limerick (National Folklore Collection.)

1946 Wren Boys bodhrán player in Athea, Co. Limerick (National Folklore Collection.)

It is believed that when St. Stephen was hiding from anti-Christian persecutors, a wren flew out of the bush that Stephen was behind and thus gave away his position. He was captured and executed. The wren is killed during the wren boy ritual, in part due to its betrayal of St. Stephen. It should be noted that similar folkloric stories exist in which wrens reveal Irish military positions by tapping on war drums during seventeenth-century campaigns against Oliver Cromwell's army and during a campaign against the Williamites (Duffy "The Wren").

Famed Irish flautist and bodhrán player Seamus Tansey offered a folkloric explanation of the wren boys. During an interview with me, he explained the origins of their ritual:

> The story behind the wren goes that the wren said he was the king of all birds, when there was a meeting of the birds after the dodo dying, that there had to be another king. The eagle came forward saying, "I'm the king of birds," so they had a chat to see which bird could fly higher up in the air, and the eagle was way up above any of them, but the wren then sat on his back and said, "You're not king of the birds. I am. I went higher." That is how the wren became king of the birds, which he didn't get fairly. So he got his payback for that. What they done is that since he was king of the birds, they sacrificed the blood of the wren for the rebirth of the sun.

During further discussion, Tansey explained and reminisced about the wren boys:

> The early origins of the wren boys came from pagan and Christian holidays coming together. The wren boys got that as kind of a second name. They were originally called the messengers from the sun that came down on the earth to bring good luck for the year. Sligo was home of the wren boys. There was no other part in Ireland like it. In my time, they were dressed in all sorts of Christmas paper, tinsel paper. They had the bodhráns with them, and they played music and they went 'round, and they used to have a little dead wren. You could hear the tin whistle above the bodhrán, miles over the bodhrán, and the flute above it, too. It was a beautiful combination to hear. It was full.

Offering a different perspective on the wren boy ritual is Limerick bodhrán maker Paddy Clancy, who described in our interview his observations of the wren boy procession during the 1960 and 1970s:

> The wren boy ritual was very prominent. There could be twenty to thirty people in each wren group. I remember going to houses on Christmas Eve and St. Stephen's Day as a part of the wren. We would have a drink, play music, dance, and collect money for charity. The wren was a great form of entertainment. People would wait for the various groups to come to their house. Activities on the night could last until 4 or 5 o'clock in the morning. There would be a big supper in the town hall, everyone eating tea and sandwiches, dancing, with twenty musicians. The wren was "the thing." People were dressed up in funny dress, usually hats and dresses. There was also a wren competition held in Listowel, Co. Kerry, each year. Groups from all over Munster would perform a music piece. There were also step dancing and singing competitions. Judges would choose the best group, and you could win up to £100.

Owen Davey described his father, famed bodhrán maker James "Sonny" Davey, and other musicians' involvement in the wren boy ritual in Gurteen, Sligo. Davey stated that his father and other musicians

> used to always go out with the wren boys, all the musicians, with straw hats on them, dressed up. You wouldn't know who was who, and they used to go to crossroad dances and céilí dances and go to the public house and have traditional music at night. It was all a go at that time, the straw boys, the wren boys, but it has died down the last few years. Not for the last five years. It doesn't seem to have been as popular for the last few years anyhow. It was

a great go there at one time for the straw boys. That's the wren boys, but I suppose a lot of those musicians have passed away. They used to be playing at sessions at that time, like Peter Horton. The straw boys used to dress up with some sort of a hat, and they used to go to different functions. They might go to dances or weddings or any house dance or party. They would dance away and would dance with all the people. And they wouldn't know with whom they were dancing because they couldn't see who they were. They used to provide their own music.

These different accounts from renowned bodhrán makers and players from around Ireland provide a glimpse into the participatory nature of the wren boy ritual. Unified by certain customs such as the bodhrán musical performance, each region of Ireland contained minor variations. Emphasized in all three observer accounts is the process of using music as a means of communal engagement during festive events. While there existed nuanced differences in the accounts provided by Tansey, Clancy, and Davey, each described the importance of musical participation and social involvement throughout the procession. The wren boy ritual provided a yearly opportunity for players to perform throughout the festivities that harkened back to the mythologized, pre-Christian origins of the drum itself.

EARLY MAKERS

Numerous personal accounts of bodhrán making and performances from the 1920s and 1930s exist that serve to dispel the erroneous notion that the bodhrán was not featured in Irish traditional music until the late 1950s. Sonny Davey from Bunanadden, Ballymote, in Co. Sligo, built his first bodhrán in 1917 and began accompanying musicians (e.g., fiddler Fred Flynn) in halls and at crossroads dances. Having learned to cure a skin from a Donegal man, he formed a workshop in 1927 and commercially produced bodhráns with the insignia "Souvenir of Ireland" for the burgeoning tourist trade (Schiller 2001, 85–86).

Before the late 1950s, bodhráns were constructed in small quantities (five to six a year) by local makers, who employed different methods of construction and skin curing. Seamus O'Kane estimated that one out of thirty bodhráns constructed would be useable. Skins could be improperly treated, stretched, and attached to the shell resulting in a skin that was too loose or too tight. "Drums were not played every night, and I would think very few of them [players] would practice. They beat heavily with a heavy stick. The skin was very thick and the surface very thick and the inside of it

Sonny Davey. (Gurteen,
Sligo, Ireland. Courtesy of
Owen Davey, 1985).

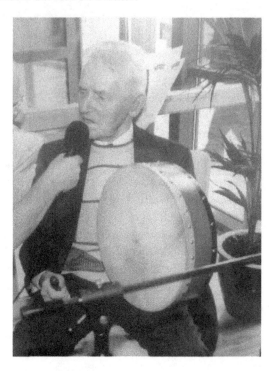

rougher again. They would use a puck goat with a skin as thick as the leather on your boot." Among bodhrán players, it was well known who possessed a good bodhrán, as only maybe twelve good drums existed in Ireland at the time. Therefore, quality bodhráns were rare and greatly sought after by players. O'Kane shared an anecdote that Peadar Mercier had offered a colleague of his more than three times the £40 value of his bodhrán because of its superior quality and scarcity (O'Kane 2015).

Sonny Davey from Co. Sligo, Paddy Clancy from Co. Limerick, and Charlie Byrne from Thurles, Co. Tipperary produced bodhráns (typically large drums with a cross bar or a wire structural reinforcement without a tuning system) for the emerging cottage industry and renewed instrumental interest (Forsthoff and Kruspe 2013, 21). It was common practice for bodhrán makers to attend fleadhs to play and sell their drums.[7] Interested customers and players would also be invited to view drums at makers' home workshops.

Owen Davey elaborated upon how his father, Sonny Davey, began crafting bodhráns.

> He started making bodhráns when he was twelve years of age. An old man had given him a bodhrán when he was around nine years of age, and then

Owen Davey with Sonny Davey's bodhrán (Gurteen, Sligo, Ireland. Colin Harte, 2015.)

he got in on making bodhráns around twelve years of age for himself. He started selling them. He used to, I remember in the early years, he used to always put jingles in it, in the rim. He'd cut out and put the jingles in. In the latter years, he used to put a cross pick [cross bar] across the bodhrán. He used to make the jingles out of an old tin of peas, or something like that, and cut the tin, cut a round circle with the jingles and just fit them in and just cut them out of a hoop and just tack them on there. Some people preferred the jingles and then the cross sticks more and more. Some of the players might not want paint at all. Some might want the skin put down more on the rim or they might not want cross sticks at all or maybe just a thumbhole in it to hold it. Mostly, the people came to the house or they got his name. His name was advertised. He'd get a letter for an order for a bodhrán. There was no phone calls. He used to travel to Clare from that time just to advertise them. People would write to him and just order the bodhrán and come when it was made, come to collect them.

Paddy Clancy discussed his entrance into bodhrán making.

I was involved in the Irish music business for a good while. I was constantly
involved in sessions of music, and I saw a market in West Limerick for the
bodhrán, as there was not a lot of producers at the time. In the 1970s people
made the bodhrán themselves. They were very cheap at that time. They
could be bought for £10 to £12. I primarily played the accordion. As I was
making and selling bodhráns at fleadhs, I took up playing it as a pastime.
People were constantly inquiring at fleadhs to see if I was selling them as they
gave a different sound to a music session — they were unique to the music
scene in the 1960s and 1970s. There were not many bodhrán producers or
players in 1970s Limerick to influence me. A good producer or player was
rare at this time, but I do remember the Sheehy brothers from Carrigkerry.
They made their own bodhráns and were in opposition to each other, always trying to outdo one another to be the better player. I suppose that is
where I first got interested to pursue endeavours with the bodhrán. Before
the 1990s, where you could have a tuneable bodhrán to vary the sound, in
the 1970s when your bodhrán skin got loose we used to put it in front of
the turf fire to tighten and tune the skin. We also used to put the corks of
lemonade bottles together and screwed them on to the rim of the bodhrán
to give different sounds. The bodhrán was first played with the back of your
hand, but bodhrán sticks became popular in the 1960s, and everyone started
making them. I never collaborated with anyone in making the bodhrán. I
wouldn't have been traveling far in those days, and collaborating wasn't a
common practice. I didn't make them for specific players either. Usually
people would hear me playing at fleadhs and ask me to make one for them.
I would make around sixteen to twenty bodhráns a year.

Charlie Byrne's bodhráns were highly regarded among players, having
supplied drums for Johnny McDonagh, Tommy Hayes, and Mossie Griffin
among others. Byrne typically built drums with diameters of 18" to 20" and
a 4" shell. He used cow manure and urine to cure the skins (O'Kane 2015).
He sold the drums from the back room in his house and stored more quality
bodhráns in his shed. Byrne also attended fleadhs in order to sell his drums.

I watched him attaching the skinhead to a bodhrán when I visited him in
Thurles. Charlie hunted wild goats in the neighboring hills for his skins.
He explained the need for bleeding them correctly so the skin wouldn't get
stained. He cured them in a warehouse at the other end of town so his family didn't have to smell them. Charlie preferred hard woods from parts of
the world other than Ireland and turned all the rims himself, sealing them
with glue. After tacking down the heads, he whitewashed the backs of the

Charlie Byrne. (Thurles, Tipperary, Ireland. Courtesy of Barbara Ryan, 1988.)

skin, which dried off relatively quickly. He described how best to clean his drums by submersing them in the bath in tepid water and gently sponging both sides of the skin. Then you "knock your wife down and pull off her pantyhose to wrap around the rim so the skin dries flat." Then you put the drum in the garage, or someplace cool, where it can dry very slowly. He said he guaranteed his drums for life.

THE EMERGENCE OF THE BODHRÁN (1950–1970)

Comhaltas Ceoltóirí Éireann was established in 1951 by members of the Dublin Pipers Club in response to the prevailing negative societal perceptions of Irish traditional music and its gradual decline in popularity.[8] *Comhaltas Ceoltóirí Éireann* created an institutional social network for traditional musicians that would eventually become international in nature and encouraged the performance and transmission of Irish traditional music.[9] The establishment of the *Fleadh Cheoil* (Irish music festivals/competitions) proved extremely successful in their revival agenda. The bodhrán was included as an instrumental category in the music competitions (Fleming 2004, 233–34). *Comhaltas Ceoltóirí Éireann* provided the groundwork to produce a successful music revival movement beginning in the 1950s.

The bodhrán regained popularity in Irish traditional music in the late 1950s to early 1960s.[10] Seán Ó Riada introduced the instrument to his group, *Ceoltóirí Chualann*, in the 1960s. He often played the bodhrán with a thick, conical tipper. The large tipper allowed for a low, resonant sound when struck against the unmuted bodhrán skin. In 1966 he replaced Davy Fallon of Castletown Geoghan, Co. Westmeath, a player in his seventies who performed on the Chieftains' first album (Glatt 1997, 54–55).

The bodhrán in Ceoltóirí Chualann was used for the same reason that the uilleann pipes, tin whistle, and Irish flute were utilized. These instruments were viewed as native Irish instruments whose timbres represented a musical culture that stretched back to antiquity. Ó Riada combined native Irish instruments and repertoire within modern ensemble arrangements in order to present a new creation that drew upon both native Irish musical culture and modernist musical concepts.

Ó Riada invited bodhrán and bones player Peadar Mercier to join *Ceoltóirí Chualann*. Cork-born Mercier would later perform with the Chief-

Seán Ó Riada and Peadar Mercier (bodhrán) performing as part of Ceoltóirí Chualann at the Gaiety Theater. (Dublin, Ireland. Irish Traditional Music Archive, copyright Gael Linn, 1969).

tains from 1966 to 1976, where he displayed an unmuted bodhrán style played with a thick tipper he had fashioned himself (Dickinson 2006, 218). Due to the enormous popularity of the Chieftains, the sound of the bodhrán was disseminated through performances and recordings. The unmuted, tipper-pounding style popularized by Mercier began to replace the quieter, unmuted hand-striking styles. This instrumental approach meant that a tipper was not used and that the tips of the fingers or knuckles would strike the unmuted drum head. The fleshy parts of the striking hand would gently mute some of the attack against the drum skin, so further muting the opposite back side of the skin with the other hand wasn't as necessary. The unmuted sound of the drum could be heard while the striking hand slightly muted the attack. The timbre of the drum changes when a thick tipper is struck against an unmuted skin, producing a large ringing tone. This timbral approach was favored by Mercier and Ó Riada.

TIPPER PERFORMANCE PRACTICES

Due to the popularity of the Chieftains' Peadar Mercier, playing styles began to shift from hand to stick. This shift marked changes in the volume, skin

Christy Moore playing the bodhrán with his hand. (Bray, Wicklow, Ireland. Courtesy of Adam Sherwood, 2018.)

Assortment of bodhrán
tippers. (New York, USA.
Colin Harte, 2018.)

attack, and timbral possibilities. The combination of stick drumming with a
largely unmuted drum skin led to loud bodhrán accompaniment that could
overwhelm the tune in indoor performance spaces. During the 1950s and
1960s, a multitude of playing styles existed.

Styles developed in which the bodhrán was struck by the hand or by a
tipper (also known as a beater, stick, striker, or *cipín*). Tippers were often
crafted from hardwoods (e.g., holly, hickory, mahogany, or oak). They were
double-headed and of various sizes and shapes (Mallinson 2007, 6). The
North Kerry style uses both ends of the double-headed tipper, as demonstrated by Frank Torpey Johnny McDonagh, and Mel Mercier.[11] The West
Limerick or top end style employs a single-end beater and is used by Junior
Davey and John Joe Kelly.[12]

The bodhrán was also played by hand (Sonny Davey, Jack Cooley,
Séamus Tansey, Christy Moore, Dónal Lunny, Ted McGowan),[13] using
the tip or knuckle of the index finger (Clare style) or the knuckles of the
hand (Roscommon style) or the thumb and pinky finger (West Cork style)
(O'Mahoney 1999, 35).

EARLY MUSICAL ROLE

The role of the bodhrán player was to provide unobtrusive, percussive rhythmic accompaniment that closely mirrored and complemented the melody. The bodhrán garnered a negative stigma in the larger Irish traditional music communities for several reasons: (1) the drum's inability to produce the pitches of melodies and thus continue the tradition; (2) the abundance of poorly constructed, inexpensive bodhráns played by unskilled players who provide disruptive accompaniment; and (3) the loud, ringing tone produced by unmuted bodhrán performance styles (Hannigan 1991, 5).

Seamus Tansey discussed with me the older role of the bodhrán in Irish traditional music.

> If you got the right bodhrán flicker, and there were great bodhrán flickers around our place, they didn't spoil the music. They uplifted it. Today you have nothing but pop drumming. You'd be as well to have Ringo Starr. Around us, we hit it with the hand; down south they hit it with the stick. A lot of them are playing stick today, and it's more like pop drumming. The bodhrán flicking is a massive beat, and it is done with the hand. I played with right bodhrán flickers, and it was lovely to play with them. They lift you up. They have a beat, and at the same time they have a basic beat and triple, both together. With the right tone on the bodhrán, it's beautiful.

Tansey further elaborated upon his bodhrán performance techniques.

> I play with the knuckle and the tip of the finger for treble. If there is a right bodhrán flicker there, he can play with you and at the same time uplift your music so your music is heard over him. If he fails to do that, then he is a bodhrán basher. I like a bodhrán flicker to play an even rhythm, a down rhythm. Not one of these bodhrán flickers that's playing a tune with you or trying to play a tune with you by pop drumming. I want a solid drum. I'll do the playing, but no fancy work. I'll do the fancy work on the flute. I follow the rhythm of the tune and do some variations now and again when I think it's appropriate, but I have to think that it's the musician that is doing the tune. He's doing the variations, so there is no need for me because the drum is a syncopation instrument. It's for time, for rhythm. If you want to do a solo and see what you are made of, that is different. But when you are playing with an instrument or a group, you are there to do a rhythm, and if you do it right and well, by god it's worth listening to.

The rise in popularity of the bodhrán was spurred on by the Irish music and folk music revivals that occurred in the 1960s and 1970s in the United

States and United Kingdom. The emergence of super groups such as the Chieftains, followed by the Bothy Band, Planxty, and De Dannan provided a professional ensemble model for Irish traditional music, focused on stage performances featuring a high degree of instrumental virtuosity. Using the older Ceoltóirí Chualann as an example, they often included the bodhrán as an ensemble instrument. These performances and recording opportunities introduced audiences to accomplished bodhrán playing, a notable example being Johnny "Ringo" McDonagh.

In the 1970s, McDonagh, who performed with the world-renowned Irish traditional group De Dannan, began placing his back hand upon the skin of the bodhrán. In this way, he was able to mute and alter the sound. Based on the position of the muting hand on the back side of the drumhead, different drum harmonics, glissandos, and variations of treble and bass could be achieved. This technique also enabled him to lower the volume, which allowed the bodhrán to better blend with the other instruments.[14] This development helped the instrument to earn a greater degree of acceptance

Johnny McDonagh muting the bodhrán skin. (Sulzemoos, Germany. Courtesy of Hedwitschak Drums, 2017.)

in Irish traditional music circles. The bodhrán was viewed at the time as a timekeeping instrument that was suitable for accompaniment but not essential to the Irish music tradition (Vallely 1999, 30–32).

The bodhrán was featured in other Celtic music ensembles during the 1970s, most notably in the Scottish bands: Boys of the Lough featuring Robin Morton, Silly Wizard featuring Gordon Jones, and the Tannahill Weavers featuring Phil Smilie. The British electric folk band Steeleye Span also included bodhrán in their music as played by Gay Woods. This period of folk music experimentation by various key players saw the inclusion of the bodhrán in new and nontraditional contexts. New microphone techniques, performance practices, recordings, and musical repertoire provided bodhrán players with limited opportunities to develop the bodhrán as an emerging ensemble accompaniment instrument.

TUNING

One of the problems that plagued bodhrán players was the inability to tune the skin and retain a steady skin tension. Due to temperature and climate fluctuations, a skin's tension could drastically change. In addition, the skin's tone would lower as the skin's tension decreased due to continued playing.

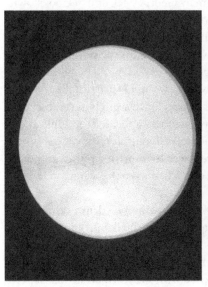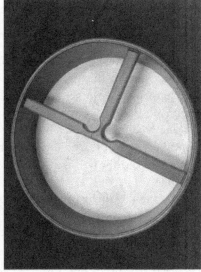

Untuned Bodhrán. (Pomona, New York, USA. Colin Harte, 2018.)

Players would attempt to adjust the skin's tension through the application of water or sometimes Guinness on the skin to slacken the skin or, conversely, warmed the bodhrán skin near a candle flame or open fire to tighten the skin. Bodhráns have become tunable due to the creation of a system by Seamus O'Kane of Dungiven, Co. Derry. It allows the player to tune the drum to a proper pitch level and maintain a more consistent, enduring skin tension. The tunable drum also allows for more clearly audible pitch slides and drum pattern articulations, which create a more suitable instrumental blend for the music.

Upon hearing a bodhrán on a recording in 1968, Seamus O'Kane, an engineering student, proceeded to build his first bodhrán. He continued to make five or six a year. In 1970, after a concert, O'Kane met with Peadar Mercier, who taught O'Kane his bodhrán construction process and made him repeat his instructions until memorized. O'Kane experimented with tuning systems, skin (types, treatments, and stretching), shell design (size, thickness, diameter, depth, and construction), and tipper design and construction. Inspired by the tuning mechanism on the outer shell of a banjo, O'Kane experimented with placing the tuning system on the inside of the bodhrán, using a tuning ring that could pull the skin down or push it up through the adjustment of screws. The ability to adjust skin tension was achieved through an eight-point tuning system that used an Allen wrench or screwdriver. Based on a tuning system by George McCann of Cookstown, Co. Tyrone (ca. 1980), O'Kane crafted an eight-point tuning system using wheels rather than pegs on the inner rim (O'Kane 2015).

O'Kane continued to experiment with tool-less tuning systems resulting in a wooden system in 1983 (*Cam Design*). He revised the eight-point tuning system, replacing the wooden tuners with gears and Delrin knobs and later switching to square finger knobs. O'Kane developed a single-screw rack and pinion tensioning system that proved to be too complicated for duplication. O'Kane finally settled on a band tensioner system that removes the tuners from the inside of the bodhrán and replaces them with a tightening band around the outside that is adjusted by one Allen wrench located on the rim (O'Kane 2015).

O'Kane was the first bodhrán maker to use lambeg drum skins on his drums, due to their thinness, sound quality, and availability in Northern Ireland.[15] O'Kane has a private process for further treating the lambeg skins whose thinness allows for greater pitch manipulation and clarity of attack. He discussed the various means of skin curing with which he has experimented. (a) Skins can be cured with lime, which is painted onto the hairy side of the skin and then the entire skin is steeped in a lime bath for twenty-three days. The hair is scraped off and washed to remove as much lime as possible. The skin is then dried for three or four days outdoors. (b) Various mixtures with lime can be applied to the skin such as those with tallow. (c) The skin can be cured with aluminum oxide powder applied to the hairy side of the goatskin. (d) Popular in Co. Sligo is the curing method of burying the skin in a cow dung hill for twenty-three days and then washing. Cow urine is also used to cure skins. (e) Oak tree bogs serve as curing sites where a hole is dug at least eighteen inches deep and the skin is submerged in the bog for five weeks. The tannic acid cures the skin (O'Kane 2015).

A similar process can be achieved by mashing two buckets of oak tree bark in water and then soaking the goatskin in it for four weeks. Tannic acid produces a bright red hue on the skin (f) Lye can be used to remove hair. (g) Burnt ash from an oak wood fire can be rubbed into the roots of the animal hair. The skin is rolled up and covered in more ash, which prevents any further decomposition. (h) The skin can also be cured with ammonia, which is painted with a four-inch brush onto the hairy side of the skin, rolled up and stored for twenty-one to twenty-three days. Skins can be weighted (stretched) by nailing them flesh side down along the outer edges to change

Seamus O'Kane with a drum size mold in his workshop. (Dungiven, Derry, Northern Ireland. Colin Harte, 2017.)

Seamus O'Kane with an early
tunable bodhrán model.
(Dungiven, Derry, Northern
Ireland. Colin Harte, 2017.)

the skin from goat shaped to a more circular shape. Adhesives such as paint
and tape can be applied to help stretch the skin. Skins can then be scraped
with a wooden or metal scraper to remove fat and to determine thickness
(O'Kane 2015).

By 1980 O'Kane was experimenting with shell design construction, and
he eventually settled on a 16" diameter, 3mm shell thickness, and 5.5" depth,
which was smaller than other bodhráns of the time. In addition to shell
design, O'Kane developed a number of bodhrán tippers crafted from hazel
wood with a uniform balancing point and 9mm in thickness, imitating the
design of a fiddle bow. Tipper designs included a thin, wooden tipper 9" in
length, split-end tippers, and the hot rod (bundled skewers with rounded
edges) (O'Kane 2015).

Driven by a desire to create bodhráns with superior sound and control,
O'Kane applied his scientific, engineering training. O'Kane's design experiments were then tested by his own musician's ear and playing. The coupling
of scientific experimentation with musicianship is a binary that would be
evident in the later works of Christian Hedwitschak, Rob Forkner, and David
Settles.[16]

COSMOPOLITANISM AND BODHRÁN
PERFORMANCE PRACTICES

Continuing through the 1980s, further performative advancements were made by Colm Murphy (*De Dannan*), Tommy Hayes (*Stockton's Wing*), Mossie Griffin, Mel Mercier, Junior Davey, and Jim Sutherland (*Easy Club*) using their ability to incorporate masterful pitch control, virtuosic stick patterns, and greater use of syncopations and rhythmic variations.[17] During an interview, Hayes asserted that he was not merely providing accompaniment but was creating a musical part that was equal to what the other instruments were playing. Influenced by percussionists from musical traditions in North Africa, Hayes mentioned the similarities between the bodhrán and the Arabic frame drum. Tommy Hayes incorporated certain Arabic hand drumming techniques into his own playing. Hayes drew parallels between an older hand style of bodhrán playing and the hand-drumming techniques involved with the Arabic frame drum. The similarities that exist in terms of the timbre of both instruments and the ability to duplicate the sounds from the Arabic drumming tradition on the bodhrán appear to be the immediate appeal for Hayes.

This cosmopolitan approach to the bodhrán repositioned the drum from its accompaniment role in Irish traditional music to a percussion instrument capable of performing in a variety of nontraditional musical contexts. The musical involvement by bodhrán players in other contexts changed the perception of the drum's role and function. Despite efforts to improve design and performance practices, players have suffered from the prevailing perception that the bodhrán is an inferior instrument due to its inability to perform melodies, its perceived, recent inclusion into Irish traditional music, and the fact that many novices to Irish traditional music are drawn to the instrument. Although organological developments have increased the expressiveness of the bodhrán, it is still often viewed by Irish music traditionalists as musically limited. Its uneasy position at the bottom of the Irish traditional music hierarchy has forced prominent bodhrán players to reevaluate their roles and relationships with Irish traditional music.

In reaction to these negative perceptions, accomplished professional players sought to legitimize the role of the bodhrán in Irish traditional music and dispel the myths surrounding the instrument. This process of seeking musical legitimacy has led to developments in instrumental design, educational practices, syncretism, and technological experimentation. University of Limerick professor Mel Mercier extended bodhrán educational practices by applying *Konnakol,* the Carnatic art of vocalizing rhythmic and percussive syllables. Due to similarities in timbre and pitch modulation capabilities between the tabla and the bodhrán, Mercier began creating syllabic representations of bodhrán patterns in order to create, preserve, and disseminate a repertoire of accompaniment and solo compositions similar to those found in the Indian classical repertoire of the tabla (Higgins 2005, 9). By equating the bodhrán with the older, established, and respected tabla tradition, Mercier attempted to legitimize the bodhrán in relation to other world music. He redefined the role of the bodhrán from superfluous percussionist to skilled accompanist through virtuosity and syncretic musical practices.

During an interview, multi-instrumentalist and bodhrán educator Steáfán Hannigan noted the similarities and influence that tabla music has had upon his own playing. Jim Sutherland (*Easy Club*) also mentioned that his bodhrán technique was influenced by the tabla playing of Zakir Hussain (*Shakti*). Rónán Ó Snodaigh (*Kíla*) musically collaborated with Zakir Hussain during the taping of TG4's *Ceolchuairt* (season 1, episode 1). In a separate interview, bodhrán player and percussionist Cormac Byrne discussed how he had imitated certain tabla attacks and pitch slides and subsequently performed percussive accompaniment on the bodhrán with British sarod player Soumik Datta and the Scottish Chamber Orchestra.

Mercier's attempts to legitimize the bodhrán within the contexts of world music and to redefine his musical role and relationship to Irish traditional music has been mirrored by Tommy Hayes. Both Mercier and Hayes have transplanted their bodhrán playing into the cosmopolitan contexts of world music in order to gain further acceptance, respect, and artistic freedom that are afforded to percussionists from other world music traditions. By attempting to redefine their Irish traditional musical roles and relationships, Mercier and Hayes sought to further the development of the bodhrán through experimentation.

Similarly, Scottish bodhrán player Jim Sutherland blended elements of syncopated jazz rhythms with Scottish and Irish reel and jig rhythms. Influenced by Scottish pipe band drum sections, Sutherland conceptualized the bodhrán as imitating the bass drum, tenor drum, and snare drum. The tuned pipe band drums produced several pitches. Sutherland was able to isolate pitches on the bodhrán by reducing overtones and eventually played simple melodies on the skin such as "When the Saints Go Marching In" during solos with Easy Club. He felt playing pitches on the bodhrán skin was akin to playing an upright bass, which he studied in secondary school. Sutherland uses a Dave Gormlie bodhrán with an early Andy Coursie tuning system with a heavy deerskin. Having fashioned a tipper from a hickory hammer handle as well as creating a heavy brush stick, Sutherland produced unusual drum timbres featuring syncopated rhythms with accented upbeat and reverse sticking patterns.[18] To accommodate his interest in the fusion of jazz and Scottish and Irish music, Sutherland wrote several tunes on the cittern for *Easy Club* to perform that incorporated syncopated jazz rhythms.

This process of repositioning Irish traditional music in relation to other traditions has resulted in traditional musicians having to navigate more complex, cosmopolitan contexts. This conceptual shift toward a cosmopolitan understanding of the bodhrán as a percussion instrument that can be utilized in various music is evident in the playing of Rónán Ó Snodaigh (Kíla), Martin O'Neill, and Cormac Byrne.[19] These players incorporate various percussive techniques and concepts from non-Irish music traditions as well as perform on the bodhrán in nontraditional musical contexts.

GLOBALIZATION AND THE BODHRÁN

A renewed interest in Irish traditional music emerged in the 1990s with the world phenomenon of *Riverdance*, the proliferation of world music including the global popularity of the Celtic music genre (e.g., Enya, Clannad), the emergence of the Celtic tiger economy in Ireland, the increased professionalization of virtuosic touring Irish traditional music groups (e.g., Flook, Danú, Dervish), and the establishment of the University of Limerick's Irish World Academy of Music and Dance (1994).

Subsequently, the bodhrán received greater attention by interested parties on a global scale, which led to greater consumer demand for bodhráns. This stimulated growth in the cottage industry of bodhrán making (both low-quality, inexpensive "tourist" bodhráns and high-quality, custom bodhráns) and witnessed a progression toward the professionalization and standardization of bodhrán production.

These custom bodhráns differed from older, shallow-shell, wide drumhead diameter bodhráns. Built by professionals, these drums were typically constructed from beech or ash wood in order to make the frame, which was usually around 8mm to 14mm thick. The frame is built around a mold, and if the wood proves to be inflexible, then a bending iron is applied. Edges of the wood are cut precisely so that the rim will fit tightly together. An internal support ring or additional rim is put around the rim, where staples or tacks can be used. A single or double cross piece can be inserted. The wet skin is then stapled or tacked to the frame and given ample time to dry. Double-sided goatskins and synthetic skins have increased the sensitivity of the bodhrán skin, making the instrument much more expressive and receptive to the player's touch. Pitch control and slides can be manipulated with greater ease and accuracy due to the improvements in design. The frame of the bodhrán has also been deepened on particular designs in order to afford the drum greater resonance. Tipper designs have flourished, offering the player a large number of choices. Each tipper is capable of producing a different sound and provides the drummer with more sonic options and creativity (O'Kane 2015).

Following in the wake of *Riverdance* and global interest in the bodhrán, a host of new makers emerged seeking to produce quality drums that could meet the increasing instrumental demands of professional and amateur players. Drawing upon Seamus O'Kane's craftsmanship and ethos of scientific experimentation and innovation, bodhrán makers such as Christian Hedwitschak, Darius Bartlett, Rob Forkner (Metloef Drums), and David Settles (Davey Drums) generated a continuous, fecund period of organological experimentation and innovation that was driven by scientific curiosity (acoustics, instrument construction and design, combination of materials, functionality), personal bodhrán performative experiences, dedicated craftsmanship, professional musical demands, emerging consumer markets, professionalization, and colleague competitiveness

Bodhrán tipper in process by Steven Moises. (Courtesy of Steven Moises. September 2, 2018.)

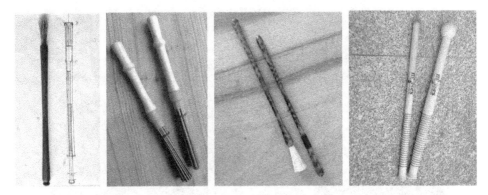

Different Steven Moises bodhrán tipper designs. (Courtesy of Steven Moises. September 2, 2018.)

SHIFT TO TOP END STYLE

As the bodhrán organologically progressed, parallel developments in performance practices occurred. In particular, bodhrán playing experienced a shift from double-ended tipper style to a top end style. In top end style, the tipper is held about three-quarters up the stick, which gives the player greater leverage resulting in more pronounced stick attack on the skin. Triplets are executed with one end of the tipper in top end style, allowing for thinner tippers to be used. As players eschewed the double-ended style, bulbous double-ended tippers were not necessary to execute triplets. Thinner tippers also allowed for a greater execution of different drum harmonics due to a reduced capacity to dampen the drumhead vibration upon tipper impact. The rise of top end style was part of larger developments in bodhrán virtuosity, accompaniment approaches, and the reconceptualization of the role of the bodhrán, which presently continues to progress.

One of the most influential proponents of contemporary bodhrán playing is John Joe Kelly of *Flook*, who uses the top end style with a thin wooden tipper, deep-shell, double-sided, taped goatskin bodhrán, one of which was built by Seamus O'Kane. His virtuosic playing exploits different tonal areas, sharp attack, and pitch slides, and features extended solo playing. He incorporates rhythms derived from drum kit patterns that are mapped onto the bodhrán. During an interview, Sandra Joyce, director of the University of Limerick's Irish World Academy of Music and Dance, noted the lasting influence of Kelly's playing upon younger players who have adopted a very similar instrumental approach and sound on the bodhrán. Kelly's

Double-ended grip. (Pomona, New   Top end grip. (Pomona, New York,
York, USA. Colin Harte, 2018.)   USA. Colin Harte, 2018.)

performance practices have been emulated by a host of young bodhrán players such as Eamon Murray (*Beoga*) and Colm Phelan (*Goitse*).

BODHRÁN NETWORKS AND INSTITUTIONS

In response to the increased interest in the bodhrán, supportive social networks and institutions were developed to address the different needs of
bodhrán players, makers, educators, and enthusiasts. In 2001 the *Craiceann*
bodhrán summer school was established. Located on the island of Inis Oirr,
Ireland, *Craiceann* (Gaelic for skin) serves as a meeting point for professional
and amateur bodhrán players, makers, and enthusiasts (Wagels "History").
In 2006 the Junior Davey Bodhrán Academy was established at the Coleman
Traditional Irish Music Centre to train aspiring players. The now defunct
World Bodhrán Championships were first held in 2006 in Milltown, Co.
Kerry. Serving as another competitive platform for accomplished bodhrán
performers in addition to the annual Fleadh Cheoil na hÉireann competitions, the World Bodhrán Championships (2006–13) centered solely on
bodhrán performance and mirrored the growing enthusiasm for the drum.

A host of bodhrán forums (e.g., bodojo.com, thesession.com) have appeared on the internet for makers, players, and educators to exchange ideas. As bodhrán organology and performance practices have developed, bodhrán pedagogy has also experienced a period of rapid development and experimentation. In particular, a wide variety of percussion notation systems and rhythmic exercises have been created by leading performers, such as Martin O'Neill and Steáfán Hannigan. A growing number of instructional videos (e.g., the Online Academy of Irish Music, Contemporary Bodhrán) and texts such as Hannigan's *Bodhrán Book* have been produced to address the growing number of aspiring players located around the globe.

CONCLUSION

By tracing the history of the drum from its early origins to present, a more nuanced understanding of the bodhrán's progression can be attained. In particular, the history of innovation and experimentation provides the context for the recent rapid alteration of the drum's structure, performance practices, and pedagogy. The rise to prominence of the drum as a versatile, customized, tunable frame drum capable of producing a wide range of timbres in various musical settings has produced new instrumental techniques, new drum technologies, and an expanding supportive bodhrán industry. Performers and enthusiasts are witnessing the transformation of the function, production, and dissemination of the bodhrán as it shifts from being a simple percussive accompaniment instrument to a dynamic, tunable, well-crafted percussive instrument capable of solo repertoire.

Notes

1. The word *bodhrán* comes from Gaelic with several associated meanings: deaf, deadness of sound, troubled, confused, numb, stagnancy of water, and unclearness and hollowness of sound or voice (Ó Bharáin 2008, 51). It is the last definition that appears to be the most appropriate and sonically accurate description of the drum.

2. The National Museum of Ireland possesses a *dallán* dating from the 1820s (McCrickard 1987, 6).

3. In the late 1930s, mechanical farm tools changed rural Irish farming and in the process made the *dallán*'s farm use obsolete. The *dallán* was then made exclusively as a drum or early bodhrán design with a somewhat thinner skin. Along the outside of the rim, pennies or bottle tops were sometimes attached to create a jingling sound similar to that of a tambourine (Hannigan 1991, 69).

4. It should be noted that the bodhrán is labeled as a tambourine on the Columbia recordings.

5. In 1947, Caoimhín Ó Danachair learned from his father, William Danaher of Athea, Co. Limerick, that the bodhrán had previously been used to provide marching music for West Limerick soldiers loyal to the Earl of Desmond (Ógáin 2002, 142).

6. For a fictional account of the wren boy processional ritual, consult John B. Keane's *Bodhrán Makers* (1992).

7. The Fleadh Cheoil na hÉireann is an Irish music competition and annual music festival organized by Comhaltas Ceoltóirí Éireann.

8. Prior to the formation of *Comhaltas Ceoltóirí Éireann*, the Dublin Pipers Club, in conjunction with the Gaelic League, had created a music festival in 1897 featuring competitions for the *uilleann* pipes (the Irish bagpipes) and the harp (Fleming 2004, 231).

9. As of 2007, *Comhaltas Ceoltóirí Éireann* claimed 36,000 members in four hundred branches located in fifteen countries on four continents (Kearney 2013, 75).

10. In 1959 the bodhrán, labeled as a tambourine, appeared in the John B. Keane play *Sive*, which won first place at the All Ireland Drama competition that year.

11. Johnny McDonagh is originally from Galway city, Ireland. In the 1970s, he developed a technique in which he muted the back of the bodhrán skin. This technique revolutionized bodhrán playing and is still in practice today. McDonagh has performed with the famous Irish traditional music group *De Dannan*. He has recorded extensively and toured worldwide. He has collaborated with tin whistler Mary Bergin and performed in *Riverdance* (Higgins 2005, 6). Mel Mercier is the son of *the Chieftains'* bodhrán player, Peadar Mercier. Mel Mercier, originally from Blackrock, Co. Dublin, began recording for the Gael Linn label during the 1970s and studied ethnomusicology at the California Institute of the Arts.

12. Junior Davey is credited with the initial popularization of the top end style, which uses the single end tipper and exploits the full tonal range of the bodhrán. He is a five-time All Ireland senior bodhrán champion (1990, 1993, 1996, 1997, 1999) and runs the Junior Davey Bodhrán Academy (formerly the Coleman Bodhrán Academy), which has produced forty All Ireland bodhrán champions in various age brackets. John Joe Kelly is the bodhrán player with the Irish traditional music group *Flook*. He is originally from Manchester, England. He has played with Irish traditional musicians such as Paul Brady and the band *Altan*. He has incorporated non-Irish traditional musical elements, and his playing is highly influential and technically virtuosic.

13. See the discography in chapter 4 for a list of recordings featuring these artists playing the bodhrán with their hands.

14. Johnny McDonagh mentioned that he practiced the bodhrán while playing along to songs on the radio. He claims that jazz and rock influenced his playing and may have shaped his decision to mute the bodhrán skin with his hand.(Higgins 2005, 75–80).

15. The lambeg drum, originating in the seventeenth century, is found primarily in Northern Ireland and is often associated with Unionists and Orange Order marches. It is typically harnessed on the neck and measures 3'1" in diameter, 2' in shell width, and 30–44 pounds. The goatskin drumheads are tightened by ropes and can produce in excess of 120 decibels (Cooper 2009, 93).

16. Rob Forkner has been playing the bodhrán since 1995. He's built drums for many of Ireland's top performers and has taught bodhrán playing and making at some of the top summer schools in Ireland and the United States. His bodhráns are custom tailored, bespoke drums fitted individually to players. He uses both traditional and exotic materials for shells and has developed drumhead preparation techniques using skins from multiple species

(Forkner 2015). Dave Settles has been making bodhráns for fifteen years in Calgary, Alberta. He is also artistic director of the Water Valley Celtic Festival (Settles 2015).

17. Mossie Griffin was the 1985 All Ireland champion on bodhrán. His single-end style playing on a Charlie Byrne bodhrán influenced younger players such as Steáfán Hannigan, John Joe Kelly, and Junior Davey. Jim Sutherland is a Scottish bodhrán player famous for his innovative drumming and blending of jazz, Scottish, and Irish traditional music in Easy Club. His use of a brush-tipper was one of the first recorded. Sutherland's drumming included pitch isolation and melody-playing on the drum skin.

18. Typical reel sticking patterns are down-up-down-up on the bodhrán. Sutherland reversed this pattern to up-down-up-down, which changes the rhythmic accents on the down strokes.

19. Cormac Byrne is a bodhrán player and percussionist from Waterford, Ireland, and is a founding member of the BBC award-winning band *Uiscedwr*. He is a principal bodhrán tutor at Newcastle University (folk and traditional music degree course) and is a guest tutor at the Royal College of Music in London and the Royal Northern College of Music in Manchester.

Two

ORGANOLOGICAL EXPERIMENTATION AND INNOVATION

From the second half of the twentieth century to the present, the bodhrán has experienced a rapid period of profound development in its construction, performance practices, pedagogy, and musical usage. A significant number of instrumental techniques and structural advances have changed the shape, sound, and manner in which the bodhrán is played. The symbiotic relationship between bodhrán makers and players spawned further advances in designs and playing techniques. As makers sought to create better sounding bodhráns in order to meet the increasing demands of players, alterations to the drumhead diameter, shell (frame) depth and curvature, drum skin treatments, and composite materials transformed the older organological models of the bodhrán.

Driven by the professionalization of Irish traditional music and instrumental virtuosity, a host of bodhrán techniques were developed and perfected including innovations in skin muting, pitch control, sticking patterns, and the mapping of various rhythms upon the bodhrán drumhead. This chapter explores many of the experiments and innovations in bodhrán design and performance practices as detailed by current makers and players.[1] The factors that motivated these developments are analyzed along with an assessment of the impact of these changes upon the future of bodhrán construction and playing.

SOCIAL CONSTRUCTION OF TECHNOLOGY

In an effort to explain bodhrán organological experiments and innovations, Trevor Pinch and Wiebe E. Bijker's social construction of technological systems (SCOT) model is employed as the theoretical framework. SCOT provides a social constructivist perspective on the development of technology. Rather than assuming that the relative success of a given technology accounts for its subsequent development, SCOT assesses the process in which a particular technology becomes repeatedly used and whose design is consistently replicated. It is essential to examine both successful and unsuccessful technological artifacts in order to assess why one design is chosen over another. Based on the uses of a given artifact, social groups select designs that best suit their technological needs. The different needs for relevant social groups can result in the creation of different designs of the same artifact or the creation of a new artifact.

The SCOT model is useful when discussing the current developmental processes associated with the bodhrán because it takes into account the different designs that have been created for amateur and professional drummers. While certain organological designs have been widely accepted (e.g., deep bodhrán shells), other developments have been less widely used (e.g., oval bodhráns).

The bodhrán's developmental process as articulated by the SCOT model consists of three major conceptual components. The first is interpretative flexibility, which posits that technological design is based on an open, continuing process of development that can produce different results based on the influence of different social circumstances. Technological artifacts can be understood as the result of negotiations between relevant social groups stemming from different interpretations of the meaning and function of the artifact (Klein 2002, 29). Therefore, drum makers can alter bodhrán designs to suit the musical needs of certain performers. The choice of materials, shape, and frame depth can be modified to produce a more appealing drum for select customers.

The second component is the concept of relevant social groups who consist of actors with similar interpretations of the meaning and function of an artifact. Assorted relevant groups can possess significantly different interpretations of a given artifact due to various group needs. A technological artifact's design can be adjusted to address a problem framed by a relevant group. As these problems may differ from group to group, different designs can arise. Thus technological development is a process in which multiple relevant groups with different interpretations of an artifact negotiate over its design, resulting in different objects (Bijker 1987, 14). Due to the different musical needs of bodhrán performers, makers have modified the materials and drum designs to achieve various acoustic properties. Bodhrán makers have altered frame depth, shape, size, and materials. Drum frames have been constructed from different woods, plastics, and metals while drum skins have ranged from kangaroo to greyhound to goat to synthetic plastics in an effort to produce different sounds. As a bodhrán's design and materials begin to significantly depart from traditional designs, new drums can be created (e.g., two drumhead bodhrán).

The third component of SCOT is the concept of closure and stabilization (Klein 2002, 30). As groups can have conflicting interpretations of an artifact, the design process continues until the artifact has resolved problems posed by each group. Closure occurs when the artifact design is no longer altered and becomes stabilized in its final form. Closure can be achieved through rhetoric or the redefinition of unresolved problems. Closure serves as a period of relative stability where the focus of discourse shifts to the acceptance and promotion of an artifact's final form by vested groups.

The concepts of closure and stabilization are expressed in the development of bodhrán tuning systems, which allow players to adjust skin tension, which regulates the pitch of the drum. Historically, tuning the bodhrán was problematic, so drum makers created various tuning systems that were progressively refined and resulted in the widespread use of hand-turned tuning knobs on the inner periphery of the drum frame. However, makers still favor other systems (e.g., Allen wrench, tuning screws) that may function better in their overall design. The standardization of tuning systems has not fully stabilized, and thus the developmental process of bodhrán tuning system design has not yet reached a state of closure.

Bodhrán makers and players are connected and access relevant drum information via communication technology (e.g., social media and internet bodhrán forums such as bodojo.com), bodhrán networking events (e.g., Craiceann), bodhrán performances, video and sound recordings, texts, and interpersonal relationships. This increased informational access and electronic connectivity has allowed for greater communication and collaboration among bodhrán makers and performers. Existing design models and performance practices can be readily imitated and elaborated upon by practitioners, allowing for the continued reproduction and reinforcement of successful models and performance techniques. As certain bodhrán design models (e.g., deep shell, tunable, double-sided goatskin bodhráns) and performance practices (e.g., single-ended tipper playing) become increasingly selected by relevant practitioners, there is a progressive shift toward the stabilization of bodhrán design. As the current state of experimentation and innovation begins to show indications of slowing, stabilization of design will occur, leading to eventual bodhrán design closure.

The bodhrán must be understood not as a single technological object but

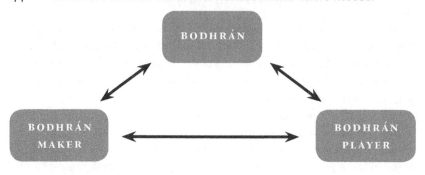

Model of Relational Dynamics.

as an instrument that has had design aspects modified over time (changes in materials, frame depth, skin treatments). The drum as a technological artifact is situated in a social web that informs aspects of its design and use. This social web of bodhrán makers, performers, and audiences influence individual and group interpretations of the drum. The bodhrán is located in a complex, fluid dynamic between drum maker technological determinism (the maker's intended uses for the drum) and performer voluntarism (the performer's decision to opt in or out of the intended uses for the drum) (Taylor 2001, 26). Each bodhrán maker discussed in this chapter reveals his own interpretations of bodhrán design and intended use, while each performer interprets the appropriate function and techniques associated with their bodhráns.

It is important to note when interpreting recent bodhrán experiments and innovations in relation to the SCOT model that a multidirectional view of the development process of the drum is taken (Bijker 1987, 11). Individual experiments in bodhrán design progress through a process of alternation between variation and selection. This results in a multidirectional model, as opposed to a linear one, in which certain innovations are acknowledged, explored, and accepted by different numbers of bodhrán players and makers in different geographical areas. Certain developments may occur in isolation and receive little attention due to a limited frequency of drum production, drum availability, and general bodhrán maker/player awareness.

While there is an informal communicative network of bodhrán makers and players, certain technological improvements gain greater social support (e.g., drum head taping) than others (e.g., noncircular drum designs) due to a host of issues dependent upon the motives of individual makers and performers. Eventually, when certain innovations are socially accepted by a considerable number of bodhrán makers and players such as deep bodhrán shells, the drum progresses to a degree of stabilization where these innovations are viewed as commonplace and part of the tradition by relevant actors.

THE DYNAMICS OF BODHRÁN
MAKER-PERFORMER RELATIONSHIPS

Central to the continued, rapid technological development of the bodhrán are the intertwined working relationships between player and maker. The triumvirate dynamic of the drum, the player, and maker is crucial to understanding the influence of one interconnected entity upon the other two. The bodhrán as a technological artifact is involved in a dynamic process in which the drum's design impacts bodhrán performance practices, while simultaneously performer interpretations of the bodhrán socially inform its function and musical uses.

During an interview, bodhrán player Mossie Griffin remarked, "The player breaks in the bodhrán, but the bodhrán also breaks in the player. There is a symbiotic relationship between the bodhrán and the player. The bodhrán is still breaking us in. That battle that I started thirty-five years ago with Charlie Byrne's bodhrán is still going on, but in a different form." Griffin was discussing the relationship between the drum and player, noting that different drums alter the manner in which a player approaches

Mossie Griffin performing on the Charlie Byrne Bodhrán with flautist Garry Shannon. (Dromoland Castle, Clare, Ireland. Courtesy of Mossie Griffin, 1994.)

Tommy Hayes with Charlie Byrne Bodhrán (Clare, Ireland. Courtesy of Tommy Hayes, 1988.)

the instrument, performs, and conceptualizes what is musically possible and appropriate for given musical contexts. He mentioned that bodhrán technology is partially driving innovations in bodhrán techniques.

The relationship between bodhrán makers and players is a crucial bond that has marked the historical development of the instrument. Discussions with Mossie Griffin and Tommy Hayes regarding their involvement with bodhrán maker Charlie Byrne revealed the connection between maker and player that was integral to ensuring the acquisition of a superior bodhrán in order to realize a particular sound on the instrument. This relational dynamic continues when players and makers collaborate to craft customized bodhráns suited to a particular player's style and specifications.

Mossie Griffin and Tommy Hayes discussed their understanding of Charlie Byrne's personality, knowing that the maker often hid his favorite and most finely constructed bodhráns from view. It took an experienced player to prod Byrne until he revealed such a quality drum. The bodhrán ostensibly serves as the central motivator for continued social interaction between maker and player. The bodhrán acquisition provided a social occurrence in which the drum intermediated between maker and player needs.

Upon receipt of the bodhrán, a period of artistic negotiation between drum and player began.

German bodhrán maker Christian Hedwitschak has developed several signature series bodhráns that were constructed based upon the specific performance needs of professional players such as Martin O'Neill,[2] Eamon Murray, Rolf Wagels, and Cormac Byrne. Hedwitschak has even created a tunable bodhrán based on the drum designs of Charlie Byrne (18" diameter drum head with 5.6" frame) along with the drum specifications of Johnny "Ringo" McDonagh (clear taped drumhead with a thick male goatskin with the spine situated two-thirds across the drum head). During interviews with O'Neill, Murray, and Byrne, each discussed having frequent conversations with Hedwitschak, where drum specifications and sonic expectations were expressed. He would then attempt to construct a drum that would reflect those requirements. Hedwitschak would mail prototypes of the drums for players to test in performances and recording sessions. These players would then provide Hedwitschak with ample feedback. This process would continue until the desired bodhrán had been produced.

The specifications of each drum vary greatly based on performance expectations. Eamon Murray's signature drum features a lambeg skin with the goat spine (a thicker part of the skin that produces a lower tone) through the drumhead's center with a tuning system and a single cross bar. Murray elaborated:

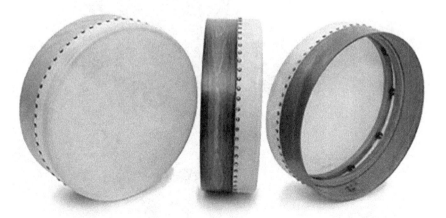

Hedwitschak TrHED Charlie Byrne Bodhrán. (Hedwitschak, September 3, 2018.)

Hedwitschak Eamon Murray's signature bodhrán. (Hedwitschak, September 3, 2018.)

Eamon Murray performing on his signature bodhrán. (Limerick, Ireland. Courtesy of Eamon Murray, 2018.)

I paired up with Hedwitschak ten to twelve years ago. I wanted something that was quick and easy to tune with a lambeg head to give more attack. He made a few prototypes and I gigged that for a while. He would send me a prototype and I would road test that for a few months and then send it back or offer some suggestions to change it. One smaller one with three tuners. Three or four different attempts, different frames, and tuning systems. We went back and forth until I got what I like. I'm still playing the prototype he sent me.

Martin O'Neill's signature bodhrán has a concave frame with a compressor tuning system, 14" in diameter and 6" shell depth, and a spineless goatskin. O'Neill explained his relationship with Christian Hedwitschak:

> I was playing a 12" drum from a guy in Wales or England, can't quite remember wherever. Christian was interested in it, curious why I was playing such a small drum. To my ears anyways, you got more of the fundamental frequency without so many of the harmonics and overtones associated with the larger frames. So for my style of playing where I was playing a lot of bass lines and pitching notes quite accurately, it really suited my style. So Christian decided to make a 12" drum and sent me one to have a go, and I fell in love with it immediately. Beautiful, really mellow tone, and the range of sounds from this drum was incredible. The bass sound on it. That really started up the relationship between me and Christian.

O'Neill discussed his involvement developing his signature series bodhrán:

> I had a solid idea of what I wanted from the drum. We sat down and discussed what I was looking for. It was a 14" model, which is a step up from the 12". In terms of skin preference, the skin used for my drum is DragonSkin Spicy. There is no dorsal line or spine from the goat on the skin. It is very even, homogeneous, and basically from every angle from every point of the drum, the skin will respond and sound the same. There is no heavier or fatter tissue. Some people like to have the spine in the middle or three-quarters to get different sounds. I like it to be even and get the same response all over. I spin the drum a lot when I'm playing, so I'm not putting so much wear and tear on one part of the skin with my left hand, which is doing all the pressure, because I use so much pressure on the back end.

Cormac Byrne's drum harkens back to older bodhrán designs with an 18" diameter, 5" shell depth, and tuning system.[3] The goat spine is positioned to the right of center and remains untaped in order to emphasize overtones. Byrne discussed his relationship with Hedwitschak:

Hedwitschak Martin O'Neill's signature bodhrán. (Hedwitschak, September 3, 2018.)

Martin O'Neill performing on his signature bodhrán. (Glasgow, Scotland. Courtesy of Martin O'Neill, 2017.)

Hedwitschak Cormac Byrne's signature bodhrán. (Hedwitschak, September 3, 2018.)

The process was he would send me one drum, and I would give him feedback via email or by phone. He would send me another one. Same thing, I would rate it in terms of top end, attack, brightness. He asked me interesting questions like: Imagine you have a mixing desk in front of you, and you have top end, bottom end, high mid, low mid, attack button, lots of different effects. Tell me where the drum is now between 1 and 10 and where you want it to be. For me that was such a great and clear way of explaining exactly what I wanted. It can be so difficult. Even when you think you are describing something, someone else might interpret it differently. Once I had the drum, I haven't gone back to any other drum since.

Influenced by the innovative designs and scientific experimentation of Seamus O'Kane, Hedwitschak has continued the experimental nature of bodhrán making, creating a tool-less, multipoint compressor tuning system with a funnel shaped, angled tuning rim intended to produce a more balanced spectrum of overtones. A leather bearing edge can be coupled with this system to reduce unwanted overtones. Hedwitschak has developed the *ChangeHed* system, which allows the players to interchange skins and light, synthetic frames through a multipoint-screw design. A variant of this design is the compact travel bodhrán (*Lillebror Trumma*). He has also produced the *DragonSkin* bodhrán, which sonically resembles lambeg drum skins and has

Hedwitschak concave frame.
(Hedwitschak, May 4, 2015.)

a concave shell. Typically, Hedwitschak shells are layered solid beech wood, but concave shells are made from the lighter cherry wood and nut wood.

In an effort to scientifically prove certain assumptions regarding bodhrán construction, Christian Hedwitschak and Dr. Rolf Wagels partnered with the University of Munich's Laboratory of Acoustics and Dynamics led by Dr.-Ing. Stefan Sentpali and funded by a European Union research grant (€20,000). In the acoustic laboratory, the bodhrán playing of Wagels was analyzed, studying the harmonic frequency response of untaped and taped bodhráns; compressor tuningrims and standard tuning rims; the addition of chamois leather to a standard tuning rim; and the variation in sound as determined by hand edge dampening. The study (one week of preparation, one week of testing, two weeks of data analysis) sought to scientifically prove commonly held assumptions that bodhrán makers and players derived from aural analysis regarding fundamental skin tones and resulting harmonics.

The Laboratory of Acoustics and Dynamics measured bodhrán reverberation duration when the perimeter of the drumhead was untaped, half taped, and fully taped. The amplitude of different harmonics was also measured. A comparative study of the fundamental tone and resulting harmonics in regard to different bodhrán tuning rim designs was conducted. Finally, an analysis of the variation of sound based on hand dampening against different areas of the drum skin was completed and will be fully published.

Hedwitschak transparent bodhrán. (Hedwitschak,
May 4, 2015.)

In collaboration with bodhrán players (Wagels, Guido Plüschke, and
Andy Kruspe), Hedwitschak has constructed a transparent, taped, tunable
bodhrán with a synthetic skin and acrylic frame intended for bodhrán instruction. Synthetic skin bodhráns have also been produced by Cooperman
Drums (Glen Velez Series). In addition, a recent collaboration between
Cormac Byrne and John Blackwell, maker of Blackwell Original Drums,
has produced a synthetic skin bodhrán with a corresponding glass slide for
greater pitch manipulation.

Blackwell began constructing tunable bodhráns with a lightweight,
paintable aluminum metal frame and synthetic skin for English Morris
dancers. Morris dances are held outside where the rain and cold can create
tuning issues for goatskin, wooden framed bodhráns. Blackwell's synthetic
bodhráns were crafted with the goal of holding their tuning regardless of
weather conditions, allowing for continuous performances. Using a six-point
tuning system requiring an Allen wrench, different types of synthetic skins
could be adhered or removed by the performer with relative ease. Blackwell
offered a hydraulic skin where a thin film of oil existed between two skins
producing a warmer drum timbre. A transparent skin and sweet spot skin,

where a snare drum power spot was adhered to the middle of the transparent skin, allowed for greater attack on the drum.

After meeting with Cormac Byrne, Blackwell encouraged the performer to test one of his drums for feedback. During an interview with Byrne, he recounted a revelatory performance experience using the synthetic drum. Searching for a tabla-inspired drum timbre during a rehearsal with *Kefaya,* a seven-piece world music ensemble, Byrne began sliding a pint glass against the back of the synthetic skin to amplify his pitch slides on the mic'd bodhrán. After the rehearsal, Byrne quickly communicated to Blackwell his discovery and demonstrated the drum's new timbral possibilities using a pint glass at a gig at the Royal Festival Hall performing alongside a tabla player. Blackwell offered to create a signature series drum with Byrne in order to capitalize on the new drum's sonic capabilities.

The collaborative drum-making process would take two and half years, requiring Blackwell and Byrne to visit each other's studios as well as exchange new drums at festivals. Feedback from Byrne was consistently sent to Blackwell as he tested new drum models. This collaboration resulted in ad-

Talking Bodhrán with tipper and slide. (Blackpool, UK. Courtesy of John Blackwell, 2017.)

Cormac Byrne performing on a talking bodhrán with slide. (Manchester, UK. Courtesy of Tom Griffiths, 2017.)

justments to the original synthetic bodhrán, including a roll on the drum's edge for comfort, a thickened drum frame (3mm) for greater resonance, a Guinness-inspired paint finish, and an aluminum pint glass. Byrne designed a custom tipper (built by Steven Moises) to be paired with the drum. In an effort to differentiate the drum from traditional bodhráns, it is called the Talking Bodhrán due to the glissando similarities to a West African talking drum.

The relationship between Blackwell and Byrne allowed both maker and performer to reconceptualize the function and timbral possibilities of the bodhrán. This process of organological adjustment and musical testing produced a bodhrán that was innovative in sound production, timbre, and construction. While Byrne views the Talking Bodhrán as a different instrument from the bodhrán due to construction, sound, and manner of playability, Blackwell contends that it is a part of the natural development of the drum. Blackwell's use of aluminum and synthetic plastics allows him to address older issues of tunability, exchangeable drumheads, weather resistance, and durability.

As globalization has increased the demand for and production of bodhráns, makers are building drums throughout the world. Older methods of bodhrán making and drum sales are changing as makers have greater access to different resources and diverse markets. This process is referred to as detraditionalization (Beck, Lash, and Giddens 1994, 2). As consumer demands and production gain importance, tradition in making bodhráns tends to decrease in significance. A gradual process of tradition erosion occurs where the cultural artifact (bodhrán) continues to be produced outside its original context, while the older tradition of making artifacts begins to be displaced and replaced by higher-grossing means of production. There exists a tension between the time-honored traditions and the more robust approach to drum production.

Historically, bodhrán making has been the pastime of select craftsmen who derived a secondary income from their drums. While bodhrán makers such as Seamus O'Kane have financially benefited, the exclusive production of bodhráns as a full-time profession is a rarity. As an exception, Christian Hedwitschak produces bodhráns as his sole profession with distributors in Germany, Ireland, Scotland, France, Spain, Belgium, Switzerland, the United States, Canada, and Japan. This dynamic shift toward the professionalization of bodhrán making and the greater production of bodhráns for international distribution represents a considerable change in the tradition and function of bodhrán making. The further professionalization has led to greater standardization.[4] During an interview, Hedwitschak discussed the creation of an affordable, high-quality, handcrafted bodhrán that could be mass-produced.

> I want to offer a product line that's high standard, but suitable for the mass of bodhrán players which is now the *Coreline,* a midrange drum line. I wanted to create a drum that is the best standard for an average bodhrán player. It is not a specific direction like the signature drums, but it is a standard bodhrán, state of the art, high quality, but not too specific in one sound direction. It is to have a high quality product at a low price.

Hedwitschak explained that while these drums are handmade, they are produced in batches of eight using standardized size models: five standard models in five sizes. He produces 550 handcrafted bodhráns each year. This vastly outnumbers the drum production of the majority of fellow bodhrán makers. As Irish traditional music has garnered international attention and appeal, the bodhrán and its production has been appropriated through the larger mass marketing of Irish traditional music and culture by the entertainment and tourist industries as articulated through music, dance, and Irish traditional musical instruments.

Other bodhrán makers such as Darius Bartlett and Rob Forkner have resisted this process of professionalization and gradual standardization. Instead, they opt to participate in the older model of bodhrán making, which focuses on the production of a small number of custom, handcrafted bodhráns at the maker's discretion for select players. Forkner explained, "I tried it full-time for a little while, and it wasn't for me. To make ends meet you have to turn out a huge number of drums, and that's not really the part that I like. Over a hundred a year is just not me. Over sixty a year is already really pushing it. I prefer twenty to thirty, which is more comfortable." The significant variations in bodhrán design from these makers can be attributed to their different interpretations of the drum's function and use. In addition, these influential actors have reconceptualized their own roles as bodhrán makers in order to accommodate their own craftsman needs and motivations.

Driven by a personal, obsessive, scientific curiosity regarding frame drum construction, composite materials, and their acoustic properties, Darius Bartlett has been building bodhráns for twenty years, often producing an individual drum solely for the purpose of experimentation. At the time of the interviews, he lived in an eighteenth-century farmhouse in France that had been converted into a workshop, filled with skins, soaking wood ash, drum shells, various woods, and even bottled feces for the purposes of goat hair removal. Bartlett explains, "I live by myself, so I can build and try a bodhrán out and measure it by all the oscilloscopes, then if it doesn't work, I put it away."

Having visited and communicated with frame drum makers in Ireland, Morocco, and Iran, Bartlett possesses a cosmopolitan understanding of the bodhrán as being part of a larger continuum of frame drums from around the world. Bartlett's custom bodhráns are sought after by players for their unique sounds and rarity. Professional player Colm Phelan apprenticed with Darius Bartlett for three months in order to gain a deeper understanding of the acoustical properties of the bodhrán and the related drum-making processes. Working closely with Bartlett, Phelan experimented with composite materials and design, even attaching a small cymbal to one bodhrán. Bartlett expounded upon the close relationship between maker and player. This relationship is important for Bartlett, who designs the drums but is not a player. "I had the opportunity to build drums for Colm that are quite different. Some of my developments have been intimately tied with his

Colm Phelan's red bodhrán
with cymbal. (Crézancy-en-
Sancerre, France. Courtesy of
Colm Phelan, 2010.)

abilities. Colm has an expansive view of the music. He has an understanding of musical space. The internal relations between musicians and sound,
that's what is interesting to me, and I have always been supportive. So in
that respect, it is a very symbiotic relationship."

Phelan has also forged a working relationship with bodhrán maker and
player Rob Forkner of Metloef Drums. Phelan spent several weeks building
a drum with Forkner in his studio in order to experiment with designs that
suited Phelan's playing. Forkner has built various drums for Phelan, seeking to produce a bodhrán that combines pronounced attack, round tone,
and longevity. Forkner has similarly collaborated with Robbie Walsh and
Niall Preston, keeping select, custom drums for these players as requested.
Forkner discussed his relationships with professional players. "My relationship with Colm, Robbie, and Niall and all those guys has definitely pushed
my making in a direction that really supports them and that was a mutual
thing. I was interested in exploiting the materials for what they're worth
and helping them amplify aspects of their playing that they wanted. It is a
challenge for me to make something that pushes them, and they give me
feedback and how that feeds into their playing."

Forkner discussed building drums that could further player techniques, based on what he heard in a select player's performances. Forkner commented on the difference between some bodhrán makers who will make a certain number of drums and have players over to their workshop to choose a drum as compared to collaborating with a player over a sustained period of time in order to produce a custom drum designed to highlight aspects of a performer's style. These interpersonal relationships with players allow Forkner to have several custom drums ready for professional players when needed. Due to the rigors of touring, Forkner mentioned that professional players like Colm Phelan would wear through several drums a year, which means he must have a custom shell and skin ready to assemble and ship in a timely fashion. This interdependence between maker and player informs the processes of drum building, performance, and the bodhrán itself.

Influenced by Darius Bartlett's experiments with bodhrán design, Forkner has used kangaroo skins (producing a mid-range heavy tone), goatskins (prepared in various manners), calfskin, and occasionally deerskin on his bodhráns, which have varied in shell depth (5" to 14"), shell composite materials (various woods, epoxies, and fibers), various shell width and shell weights, and detailed, decorative shell laminations and inlays. Forkner's deep shell drums (12" to 14") resulted from a desire to gain greater tonal directionality from the bodhrán when mic'd on stage. Forkner has also

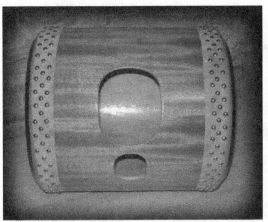 

A. Double headed bodhrán design. B. Deep shell bodhrán design. (Metloef, May 14, 2015.)

A. Currach bodhrán design.
B. Hooker bodhrán design.
C. Plassy bodhrán design.
(Daveydrums,
May 14, 2015.)

produced a double-headed, separating 14" shell depth bodhrán on which two players could perform at once.

Forkner's experimentation and collaboration in bodhrán design has not been limited to professional performers. Working with Canadian bodhrán maker and player David Settles, Forkner agreed to produce a drumhead for an oval bodhrán, and Settles would produce the shell. Settles has produced a variety of unorthodox bodhráns (oval, teardrop, figure-eight) in order to test comfort, playability, tone production, and design structure. Settles favors the teardrop *Plassy* design due to his ability to produce a wider variety of hand shapes against the back surface of the drum. Settles has also experimented with beaver skin for drumheads and the use of oak and Baltic birch for bodhrán shells. Settles performs regularly in Calgary.

CONCLUSION

Evident in bodhrán making and playing are the relational dynamics that stimulate experimentation, innovation, professionalization, and standardization. The interconnectedness between the relevant social groups (bodhrán maker and player) and technological artifact (bodhrán) allows for a rapid flow of information concerning designs, acoustics, conceptualizations of the drum, aesthetics, functionality, and critical feedback that drives instrumental development. Despite initial efforts to professionalize and standardize production, the drum is still in its developmental stages in which the majority of bodhrán makers handcraft drums for select bodhrán-soliciting players. Participants are presently witnessing bodhrán organological change at a rate that exceeds current equivalence elsewhere in the tradition. These developments are being disseminated through international networks of players, makers, educators, enthusiasts, and instrumental distributors who are changing the nature and function of the bodhrán as we know it.

As the drum is being reconceptualized by bodhrán makers and performers alike, its design has yet to reach a state of closure. The overall frame drum design of the bodhrán has reached a point of relative stabilization. However, due to the wide range of experimentation concerning frame depth, drumhead size, materials, and sound production, the drum's design must endure past the current period of experimentation and transition into a continued period of little to no change in the bodhrán's design.

Notes

1. See the bibliography for a full listing of bodhrán makers and players whom I interviewed.

2. Martin O'Neill of Glasgow, Scotland, won an All Ireland bodhrán title in 2002. He has worked with Stevie Wonder, Béla Fleck & the Flecktones, Julie Fowlis, Danú, and Fred Morrison and the Treacherous Orchestra. Eamon Murray from Randalstown, Co. Antrim, has held the All Ireland Bodhrán title on four occasions. He cofounded the Irish group *Beoga,* and he has performed with many renowned artists including Solas, Cara Dillon, the BBC Ulster Orchestra, Brian Finnegan, Liz Carroll and John Doyle, Kevin Burke, Laura Cortese, and Mícheál Ó Súilleabháin. Dr. Rolf Wagels has been playing the bodhrán since 1993. He performs with the band *Cara* and teaches in Germany, Ireland, and the United States. He has consulted with Christian Hedwitschak regarding the compressor tuning rim and the Coreline model and has coproduced a Hedwitschak bodhrán signature line.

3. Bodhrán makers such as Brendan White continue to make tunable, quality older model drums for players such as Johnny McDonagh, Dónal Lunny, Kevin Conneff (the Chieftains) and Colm Murphy. White employs a host of bodhrán-making techniques such as double goatskins for greater pitch manipulation, hollow rims with ten holes for greater resonance and volume, and a groove rim, which allows for a greater hold on the drum.

4. In interviews with Christian Hedwitschak and Darius Bartlett, they discussed patents held on bodhrán designs and composite materials, which is a recent development in the professionalization and standardization of bodhrán making. Patents are polemical for bodhrán makers as they can serve to protect the emerging bodhrán cottage industry or can hinder further developments.

Three

PERFORMANCE PRACTICES

Once at Glastonbury Festival, I was playing solo on the Main Stage on Sunday afternoon. I played a very long bodhrán solo and, I swear, the crowd grew from 10,000 to 30,000 when the sound man dropped in the sub bass halfway through. Nearby cows stopped grazing momentarily, and two women gave birth prematurely.

— Christy Moore

INTERPRETATIVE MOVES

The concept of interpretative flexibility accounts for the different ways in which performers conceive and produce sound on the bodhrán. These different interpretations of the role of the bodhrán performer and the means with which to produce different drum timbres has led to a wide variety of experiments and innovations in performance practices. Chapter 2 examined the influence of bodhrán maker-performer relationships on bodhrán design. This chapter explores the relational dynamics between the performer and the bodhrán. Based on the performer's understanding of his musical role and desired drum timbres, the percussionist will apply different materials (various tippers, metal slides, and music electronic technologies), rhythmic patterns, and contextual performance practices to the bodhrán. The performer shapes his sound through his understanding of applied materials, rhythmic patterns, and musical interactions in an effort to achieve a desired musical performance. Building on the bodhrán maker's intention for a certain range of timbral possibilities, the performer seeks to manipulate and enhance the drum's sonic palette. The drummer interprets the bodhrán in a certain manner and acts upon the drum with an audiated musical outcome. In turn, the bodhrán's design, materiality, and range of timbres can offer different possibilities for sound production. For example, a small bodhrán with a 14" diameter and a synthetic skin drumhead with a resonant, tunable metal frame can provide different musical possibilities (timbre, rhythmic patterns, accompaniment, musical contexts, musical roles) than a bodhrán with a taped 18" diameter drumhead, deep shell, and goatskin. These interpretative choices or moves greatly impact the performer's approach to the drum and audiation of it.

Interpretative flexibility dovetails nicely with Steven Feld's discussion of interpretative moves. Interpretative moves are a theoretical framework that explains the processes a musician goes through as he experiences and makes sense of a musical event or artifact. Feld posits that one cannot engage with a musical event or artifact without simultaneously experiencing the musical reality and relating it to an extramusical reality structured and informed by the interaction and culmination of sociocultural experiences. Thus we cannot interact with a musical event or object without connoting previous musical experiences. The continual construction of interconnections between these musical experiences shapes our musical expectations, aesthetics, audiations, and musical intellection.

This process of interpretation is compounded by our own sociomusical experiences, musical background, and performances. A performer encounters an instrument or event and proceeds to make musical and extramusical associations. The instrument embodies certain maker intentions through its design as well as perceived musical expectations. The performer must continually navigate a host of musical and extramusical experiential associations while engaging with the musical instrument and musical event. The interpretation of a musical instrument/event involves understanding the web of relationships that exist among musical structures and contexts. This process of navigating these different associations and acting upon them can be labeled as interpretative moves (Feld 1984, 7–8).

Interpretative moves involve the ways in which we interact with and make sense of a musical experience. Feld argues that we filter the musical experience through five parameters: locational, categorical, associational, reflective, and evaluative. Locational involves comparing a musical experience with similar musical experiences within a certain range. Categorical involves grouping musical experiences into defined sets. Associational relates a musical experience to other related stimuli, both musical and nonmusical. Reflective relates the musical experience to personal or social conditions, and evaluative involves passing a value judgment on the musical experience itself. These five interpretative moves are not equally represented in each listening experience (Feld 1984, 9).

These interpretative moves occur as musicians begin to make sense of a musical event. Upon engaging with a bodhrán, a performer may make a locational move where he/she connects the bodhrán with similar frame drums and their related techniques (e.g., the tar drum). The performer may make a categorical move by relating the bodhrán to Irish traditional music. An associational move may occur in which the performer relates the bodhrán to particular visual, musical, or verbal imagery such as an Irish traditional music session in a pub. A reflective move can occur when the musician reflects upon similar performances such as how other musicians have communicated and performed at particular sessions in the past. Finally, a performer may make an evaluative move in which he determines whether a certain musical object/event is enjoyable, funny, inappropriate, or distasteful (Feld 1984, 8–9). While these interpretative moves can happen with different frequencies and sequences, they provide a useful theoretical framework for analyzing the experiments and innovations in performance practices as realized by other bodhrán players.

OLDER ROLE OF THE BODHRÁN AND PERFORMER

In order to better understand the interpretative moves made by musicians, it is necessary to detail the prescribed and reinvented musical roles of bodhrán performers. In recent years, there has been a marked shift in the perception of suitable roles leading to a pluralistic understanding of how and what a performer can play in relation to other musicians, Irish traditional and nontraditional alike. This reconceptualization of the possibilities for the percussionist's role and musical contributions has significantly impacted the interpretative moves made by drummers. As bodhrán performers rethink their musical roles and manner of participation, drummers are recalibrating the way that they interpret, situate, associate, and eventually evaluate the bodhrán in relation to other aspects of music. By analyzing older and newer models of percussionist musical roles, a better understanding of the musical choices made by performers in relation to accompaniment patterns, musical selections, musical structures, the incorporation of nontraditional music, and the application of musical technologies to the drum can more easily be achieved.

As outlined in chapter 1, the bodhrán has always played an accompanying role. Whether the instrument is tapping time at a harvest festival or playing a tune along with other instruments at a session, the bodhran's percussive nature can enhance a musical event with its ability to create a sense of lift in the rhythmic patterns and to offer an assortment of timbres.

As musical roles are relational, the traditional role of percussive accompanist situated the bodhrán performer in a low-status position in the greater hierarchy of Irish traditional music. The tradition has always prized highly skilled melodic instrumentalists capable of performing and continuing the cultural heritage constituted in the vast repertoire of tunes. Some Irish traditional musicians view the bodhrán as a simplistic and inferior instrument, in part, because bodhrán players are not required to learn and memorize tunes in the same fashion as melody players and chordal accompanists. It is this erroneously perceived lack of investment in the tradition itself and the inability to melodically perform and continue the musical core of the tradition (the tunes) that have positioned the bodhrán at the bottom of the Irish traditional hierarchy. These perceptions of the bodhrán exist in both Ireland and Irish diasporic communities.

From their initial involvement in Irish traditional music, bodhrán players were not always accepted, respected, or wanted. This is partly due to the fact that many did not mute the back of the skin with their hand and thus played the drum in a loud, resonant manner. This was further exacerbated in the late 1950s and early 1960s when bodhrán players began playing the drum with a thick tipper and unmuted skin, inspired by Peadar Mercier. As indoor sessions grew in popularity and became the locus of Irish traditional music performances, loud, unmuted bodhrán playing associated with outdoor performance (e.g., wren boys procession) came to be viewed negatively because the performance context shifted almost exclusively indoors (e.g., pubs, houses, dance halls, and concert halls). The bodhrán was viewed as a relatively abrasive instrument that did not necessarily blend well with the other instruments (Hannigan 1991, 5–15).

Further compounding this negative perception of the drum is the fact that for Irish traditional music novices, the bodhrán can serve as an easy access point for learning and performing while socializing with fellow musicians. While melody players are expected to aurally memorize a large repertoire of tunes in order to participate in a session, a beginning bodhrán player is simply expected to know the basic rhythmic patterns of Irish dance forms (e.g., jig, reel, hornpipe). Free from the burden of performing repeated, complex, and often rapid melodies, the bodhrán player rhythmically accompanies lead melody performers. Through percussive accompaniment, bodhrán players can learn the fundamental concepts and aesthetics surrounding Irish traditional music without the pressures of melodic performance. Due to the abundance and affordability of mediocre bodhráns, Irish traditional music novices frequently utilize this method of cultural engagement.

The bodhrán is a relatively new addition to Irish traditional music and still in a developmental stage in which experimentation is rampant. Despite efforts to provide new educational methods and improve performances, players have suffered from the prevailing perception that the bodhrán is an inferior instrument due to its inability to perform melodies, its recent inclusion into Irish traditional music, and the fact that many novices to Irish traditional music are drawn to the instrument. Although organological developments have increased the expressiveness of the bodhrán, it is still viewed by Irish music traditionalists as musically limited. Its uneasy position at the bottom of the hierarchy has forced prominent bodhrán players to reevaluate their musical roles and relationships with traditional music.

This older model of the role of the bodhrán informed players' concept of the musical application, possibilities, and means of musical participation in Irish traditional music and beyond. A performer's interpretive moves were governed by this role of limited percussive accompanist. This model located the bodhrán and its performer in a low hierarchical position in the tradition; suggested the performance of unobtrusive, melody-following rhythmic accompaniment in a secondary musical role; and indicated that the bodhrán was an inferior, limited drum suitable only for Irish traditional music. This restrictive role and cultural perception of the bodhrán began to be challenged by experienced bodhrán performers as Irish traditional music enjoyed a cultural revival in the 1960s and 1970s. As players began to practice with traditional and nontraditional music, bodhrán practitioners began to experiment with new timbres and techniques leading to a questioning of this older musical role. While Irish traditional ensembles such as the Chieftains and De Dannan featured skilled bodhrán performers, drummers sought to reconceptualize and reposition their own musical role within the tradition and within the greater world of music. This rethinking of the role of the bodhrán would adjust the parameters of each player's interpretive moves.

This is exemplified in the sentiments of De Dannan bodhrán player Johnny McDonagh, who recounted that in the 1970s he felt a certain sense of rejection from other traditional musicians, which conflicted with his self-perception of being a traditional musician. McDonagh identifies himself as an Irish traditional musician who also plays in other musical contexts. He views the bodhrán as a rhythmic timekeeper that can enhance the music. It was McDonagh who pioneered drum muting by placing his hand on the back of the drum, which alters its sound. This technique also enabled him to lower its volume, which allowed the bodhrán to better blend in with other instruments. This development helped the instrument to gain greater acceptance in Irish traditional music circles (Higgins 2005, 80–82).

McDonagh commented that the bodhrán is a highly underrated instrument that is capable of equaling such instruments as the conga or talking drum. Johnny McDonagh discussed his ability to imitate percussion techniques from other cultures as well as to create effects that other drums are incapable of producing (e.g., glissando). McDonagh's instrumental technique and refined expressiveness discourage the older view of the bodhrán as an abrasive musical instrument (Higgins 2005, 80–82).

In an interview with Dermot Sheedy, bodhrán player and percussionist (Éalú, Hermitage Green, Beoga, Ciorras, Kilfenora Ceili Band), he explained that if he were playing the bodhrán in an Irish traditional music session, he would perform as an accompanist and would not include nontraditional techniques. He said that he would alter his playing style in order to blend in with the other musicians and to maintain a specific musical aesthetic set by them. He added that when he was playing with traditional musicians who appreciated nontraditional innovations, he felt comfortable experimenting with new techniques. Sheedy performed in an Irish traditional music band, Éalú, which incorporated nontraditional music concepts such as 7/8 meter. In such a musical environment, he felt comfortable utilizing newer bodhrán techniques that he felt would be musically inappropriate for traditional music sessions.

Sandra Joyce, bodhrán player and professor for the University of Limerick's Irish World Academy of Music and Dance, further supported this sentiment by stating that she felt that her role as bodhrán player was as an accompanist. She would listen to a tune being played, and her bodhrán playing was then intended to rhythmically support this tune. Joyce also mentioned that musicians would influence her traditional accompaniment approach, and they would also expect a certain type of accompaniment. She said that bodhrán players should be aware of both traditional and nontraditional accompaniment approaches. She said it was also important for a bodhrán player to understand when the traditional and the nontraditional roles are musically appropriate.

RECENT ROLE OF THE BODHRÁN AND PERFORMER

As articulated in the history of the bodhrán in chapter 1, bodhrán players such as Colm Murphy (De Dannan), Tommy Hayes (Stockton's Wing), Mossie Griffin, Mel Mercier, Junior Davey, and Jim Sutherland (Easy Club) began challenging the older musical role of the bodhrán. Looking at nontraditional music with established percussion traditions (e.g., jazz drumming,

Colm Murphy. (Dublin, Ireland. Courtesy of Colm Murphy, 1996.)

Junior Davey. (juniordaveybodhranacademy.com, September 3, 2018.)

Indian classical tabla music, North African frame drumming), percussionists drew from music of the world in order to redefine their own musical roles within the broader realm of percussion as well as within Irish traditional music. The reconceptualization of the possible musical roles and percussive participation in traditional and nontraditional contexts led to the gradual

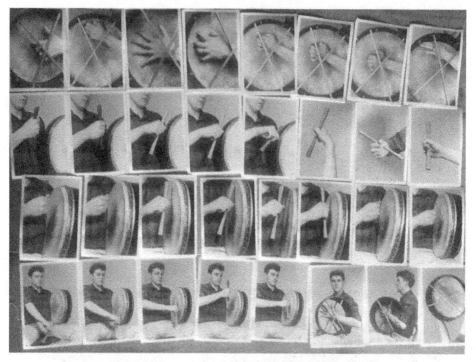

Jim Sutherland. (Glasgow, Scotland. Courtesy of Jim Sutherland, 1990.)

shift in perception of the bodhrán by practitioners. This continual process of remolding the musical role and performance practices of the bodhrán was later adopted by players such as Rónán Ó Snodaigh (Kíla), Martin O'Neill, and Cormac Byrne.

   This reconceptualization of the musical possibilities for the bodhrán altered players' interpretative moves. The locational move benefits from a wider range within a subjective field (e.g., musical experiences) resulting in the repositioning of the bodhrán in terms of traditional hierarchy, instrumental primacy, and musical traditions. This new model tells the performer to change a categorical move by relating the bodhrán to music of the world, well outside the domain of Irish traditional music. An associational move may occur in which the performer relates the bodhrán to different models of percussive roles. A reflective move can result in a performer deciding to draw upon nontraditional musical techniques (e.g., applying a hollow metal slide to the back of the drum skin or employing North African hand drum techniques) in an effort to establish new musical participatory practices.

Rónán Ó Snodaigh (Dublin, Ireland. Courtesy of Rónán Ó Snodaigh, 2018.)

Finally, a performer may make an evaluative move in which he determines that the older musical role model is distasteful and excessively restrictive, leading to a rejection of the older model and construction of a newer, inclusive model for the role of the bodhrán.

Through the reshaping of the bodhrán's role, a more pluralistic understanding of its musical possibilities was developed and communicated to players. These percussionists have to navigate the traditional musical expectations, new opportunities for experimentation, and nontraditional musical appropriations. As bodhrán players in Ireland and abroad are exposed to both Irish and non-Irish music, they must sift through this abundance of musical information and construct a musical aesthetic that represents their concept of what constitutes Irish traditional music. The reconciliation of Irish traditional music and non-Irish music is a process of cultural negotiation that addresses issues of assimilation, relocation, and the flow of information between musical communities. Since each bodhrán player must choose between different musical influences, it is useful to analyze the manner in which selected players have participated in this process.

One of the catalysts in advancing bodhrán performance practices is the increasing professionalization of Irish traditional music. In particular, the marketing, recording, and touring of progressive Irish traditional music

ensembles (e.g., Danú, Beoga, Goitse), structured around three or four melodic instruments and two or three accompaniment instruments, has led to
changes in bodhrán performance practices. Building upon Seán Ó Riada's
concept of the Irish traditional music ensemble, the dynamic of melody instruments (e.g., flute, tin whistle, accordion, fiddle, uilleann pipes) coupled
with the rhythm section (e.g., bodhrán, guitar, bouzouki, piano) has often
produced modern arrangements of Irish traditional tunes or group-penned
tunes that harken to a rock or jazz band concept of orchestration.

Within the contexts of an Irish traditional ensemble, this means that the
bodhrán functions as the drummer who syncs his playing with the other
harmonic accompanists and melodic performers. As the primary performance space for these professional ensembles is the concert hall stage, new
developments in bodhrán performance practices have emerged regarding the
mapping of different sonic regions of the bodhrán in a manner akin to the
drum kit. As percussionists conceptualize different bodhrán sonic regions
in relation to the drum kit (e.g., bass bodhrán timbre to a kick drum hit),
variations of drum kit notation have been used to articulate with greater
specificity certain bodhrán technique and timbres. Western art music compositions for bodhrán have been written, and there is a growing live focus
on the evolving bodhrán solo during concerts. These performance practices
arise from the shift to concert hall ensemble performances, a greater em-
phasis on the rhythm section, extended drum solos, and the employment of
drum notation, which are more akin to jazz or rock than earlier solo forms
of Irish traditional music.

Many of the younger professional bodhrán players have studied and are
proficient in other percussion traditions as part of their musical training.
This polymusicality has led to a greater cross-pollination of musical thought.
Players such as Cormac Byrne and Martin O'Neill studied orchestral percussion and drum kit in undergraduate classes, while Eamon Murray (Beoga)
and Colm Phelan (Goitse) studied bodhrán as well as other percussion traditions and instruments at the University of Limerick's Irish World Academy
of Music and Dance. Through academic exposure to different percussion
traditions, drum notation, and drum kit techniques, the inevitable inclusion
of certain nontraditional percussion concepts have been incorporated into
bodhrán performances.

Drawing upon notions of ensemble interplay and nontraditional drumming traditions, bodhrán performers such as John Joe Kelly (Flook), Rónán
Ó Snodaigh (Kíla), Eamon Murray, and Colm Phelan have increasingly
mapped drum kit beat patterns onto the sonic ranges of bass, mid, and

treble on the bodhrán's drum skin. While this practice goes back to Johnny McDonagh's discussion of incorporating a rock back beat for reel accompaniment, there has been significantly greater attention spent on assigning the drum kit's bass drum to the bodhrán's bass region, tom-tom patterns to the midrange, snare drum patterns to the midtreble range, and using brush and hot rod tippers to achieve a musical approximation of a high hat.

Martin O'Neill further elaborated on the relationship between drum kit and the bodhrán:

> When I was in school I had much more formal music education where I learned to read and write music and I studied drum set, percussion, and piano. I went on to do a university degree in music, which covered a big spectrum — classical music, jazz, funk, pop, rock — and at the same time I was doing trad on the side. I started to realize I could marry the two together. I realized a lot of the drum set technique and percussion technique were quite easy to transfer onto the bodhrán. Things like double strokes for syncopated rhythms seemed to be very natural. My actual grip came from a cross between traditional grip, jazz drumming, marching band, pipe band drumming, and less wrist movement. I took as much from that as I could and applied that to the bodhrán. In terms of voicing, outside of the trad community the music I created was inspired by drum set rhythms for a start, thinking of voicing, my low note or open note being in place of a kick drum, and my high note being in place of a snare and the muted notes in the middle, the clicky percussive notes being like the high hat. Realizing that all these rhythms fell under my hand very easily, it changed my approach to the bodhrán.

Apparent in O'Neill's discussion of the fluidity between drum kit and bodhrán techniques is the musical realization of the bodhrán as the cosmopolitan percussive, rhythmic center of the modern Irish traditional music ensemble. Similar to the role of the drum kit in jazz, rock, and funk, the sonic versatility of the bodhrán lends itself to fulfilling a more polyrhythmic percussive role where several percussive patterns are being executed at once (e.g., high hat, snare, tom-tom, and kick drum).

O'Neill explained that over the past few years, he had developed a hybrid drum notation. Initially he copied standard drum set notation, so that a drum kit rhythm would be assigned a low, middle, or high note. If O'Neill were writing drum exercises where pitch didn't matter, he would use single line notation like orchestral snare drum notation. However, recently he developed a bodhrán notation system, so that the notes on the stave have different sized note heads. Smaller note heads indicate ghost notes, and accented notes have an accent sign above them. Slurs are used to indicate pitch bends and where a note starts and finishes.

In an interview with Cormac Byrne, he analytically discussed how in the "mid- to late 1990s, John Joe Kelly was developing the drummer role and the groove style approach to playing. The bodhrán was higher in the mix than it previously was and became a featured soloistic type and so for this type of drummer approach, bass drum, snare drum, hi-hat sound, the taped drum is ideal for this really." Building upon John Joe Kelly's drum kit–inspired bodhrán playing, Byrne described practicing the bodhrán using percussion method books in order to develop dexterity. Byrne further elaborated that the drum kit notation he appropriated for the bodhrán served as a general musical guide, which prepared him for future gigs in which he performed in nontraditional contexts in which a basic drum score was provided.

Further deepening the relationship between drum kit and bodhrán in an ensemble format, Cormac Byrne has situated the bodhrán as the percussive center of his larger drum kit. Inspired by the work of Trilok Gurtu, who placed the tabla as the center of his world music–inspired drum set, Byrne

Cormac Byrne with bodhrán and drum kit. (Manchester, UK. Courtesy of Tom Griffiths, 2017.)

performs on the bodhrán surrounded by an interchangeable drum kit consisting of ride cymbals, high hat, bass drum, shakers, tambourine, and cajón. Evident in his live and recorded work with the folk trio Uiscedwr and jazz trio Five Countries, Byrne has fully incorporated the bodhrán as part of his cosmopolitan, world music–inspired approach to percussive performance. In the process, he has further distanced the drum from its earlier musical role in Irish traditional music, while fully embracing the timbral and orchestral possibilities of various percussion traditions.

The discussion of shifting performer interpretative moves is relevant in an effort to more fully understand the spectrum of bodhrán musical thought and performance. Through exposure to different musical traditions, polymusicality, and cosmopolitan music education, younger generations of bodhrán performers are relocating, categorizing, reflecting, and reevaluating older Irish traditional models of percussive accompaniment. In the process, professional bodhrán performers are shedding older restrictive musical roles and reenvisioning the musical usage of the drum in experimental formations within an ensemble format.

John Joe Kelly on bodhrán. (Seamus O'Kane, May 14, 2015.)

Driven by the theatrical demands of a touring professional Irish traditional music ensemble, the bodhrán solo began to evolve as each instrumen-
talist presented a stage approximation of a masterful musical party piece.
The earliest recorded bodhrán solo can be heard on De Dannan's *Selected Jigs,
Reels & Songs* album (1977) as performed by Johnny McDonagh. Inspired by
jazz drum solos, Jim Sutherland furthered the live bodhrán solo in his percussive work with his Scottish jazz-folk fusion group Easy Club. However, the
bodhrán solo became a staple of the professional Irish music ensemble with
the technically virtuosic bodhrán performances by John Joe Kelly (Flook).
As bodhrán players accessed solos via the internet, the bodhrán solo was
quickly adopted as part of the stage performances of younger modern Irish
traditional music ensembles (e.g., Danú, Beoga, Goitse).

Bodhrán solos are marked by the individual focus afforded to the drum,
hitherto nonexistent. A primacy is granted to dexterous virtuosity, a musical exploration of the sonic ranges of the drum, a demonstration of different timbres via tippers and hand techniques, and the execution of multiple
rhythmic patterns. Primarily absent from session and home performances,

Brian Fleming performing with a metal slide. (Dublin, Ireland.
Courtesy of Hegarty, 2017.)

the bodhrán solo has become a marker of the professional, stage-worthy bodhrán performer, as an abundance of technically brilliant solos are made available online.

Brian Fleming has furthered the bodhrán solo by composing a theatrical percussive piece entitled *The Day the Apaches Rode into Vietnam*. Inspired by the film *Apocalypse Now* and cowboy television series, the composition is replete with brush-tipper whirring sounds approximating the sounds of a helicopter, a horse-galloping rhythmic pattern, a rim shot, pitch slides, and rapid Senegalese djembe-inspired hand drumming on the upper portion of the bodhrán drumhead. This creative rendering of the bodhrán solo illuminates the many artistic avenues that are now being explored.

In conjunction with affording the bodhrán greater instrumental primacy is the work of Steve Forman. His extended career as a studio percussionist, touring musician, and western art music composer eventually led to his focus on the musical adaptability of the Irish frame drum. Inspired by the drum's versatility and recent introduction into the realm of world percussion, Forman sought to compose chamber ensemble and orchestral works that prominently featured the bodhrán. Often these compositions are couched in a twentieth-century approach to chamber music writing, devoid of the familiar trappings associated with Irish traditional music. The bodhrán is tasked with providing a complex web of percussive accompaniment for technically demanding scores. Works such as *Don't Wait Up* (2006) for chamber ensemble, *The Clydean Coronaries* (2008) for brass, Scottish highland pipes, and drum, and *Hameward Bend* (2009) for full orchestra represent a considerable departure from the drum's earlier musical roles in Irish traditional music and hints at the enormous potential for musical growth.

APPLIED MUSIC TECHNOLOGIES

Further extending the percussive palette, music technology has been used to enhance and alter the sound of the bodhrán. Music technology has varied, ranging from the application of a metal slide against the back of the drum skin to mic'ing the drum and processing the sound through effects pedals. For the purposes of this research, "technology consists of those material objects, techniques, and knowledge that allow humans to control the inanimate world" (Westrum 1991, 7). Technology can be defined more concisely as the "application of organized knowledge" (Mack 1997, 79). In relation to the bodhrán, music technology can be subdivided into technology that uses an acoustic application (e.g., metal slide against the drum skin) and technology that employs an electronic application (e.g., microphone or effects pedal).

Beginning with the advent of recordings, technology has become increasingly inseparable from music itself. Music technology can no longer be viewed as simply machinery that imitates or documents pre-formed music. Advances in music technology — recording equipment, computer editing abilities, multitracking, digital effects, overdubbing, amplification, microphones, sampling, radio, and the internet — have created a situation in which technology is an element of music making (Penley and Ross 1991, 254).

ACOUSTIC APPLICATION

One of the earliest music technologies acoustically applied to the bodhrán was the tipper. Carved from various woods, the density of the tipper resulted in different sounds when hit against the skin. Eventually hotrod tippers and brush tippers (first designed by Jim Sutherland) resulted in greater timbral variety. The vast assortment of tippers that exist allows for performers to adjust the drum's sound based upon the music.

Rónán Ó Snodaigh playing bodhrán with a slide. (Dublin, Ireland. Courtesy of Rónán Ó Snodaigh, 2018.)

In the 1970s Johnny McDonagh taped the outer rim of the drumhead in order to dampen ringing overtones, which altered the physical drum and its sound through applied acoustic technology. The taped drumhead coupled with the hand muting of the back of the drum skin represents a further effort to adjust the drum's timbre through simple yet effective technological means.

In an effort to further accentuate the bodhrán pitch slide, Rónán Ó Snodaigh placed a hollow aluminum tube against the drum skin. The timbre produced from the metal tube was akin to the pitch slides heard from a tabla or talking drum. Ó Snodaigh explained to me, "I began playing what they call the slide bodhrán, and it was really an invention of my brother's. He was cutting holes into the pipe to make a flute out of it. I thought it could work well on the back of the bodhrán, and I put my fingers on the holes and I could get different notes out of it. Then I tried it and it got a 'woowoo' sound and I've been messing about with it ever since." Inspired by Ó Snodaigh, Cormac Byrne has adapted an aluminum pint glass that he applies to a synthetic skin bodhrán, which he has named the Talking Bodhrán.

ELECTRONIC APPLICATION

Seeking to enhance or alter the bodhrán's sound, players have been incorporating affordable electronic technologies such as microphones, effects, synth drums, and drum loops into their performances and recordings. Donal Lunny, the *Planxty* multi-instrumentalist, has reported using an AKG D112 kick drum microphone for live performances to increase the bass presence of his bodhrán playing. Bodhrán glissandos and bass levels are exaggerated to create a musical presence in Irish traditional music that was previously unachievable in an acoustic setting. Lunny's technological experimentation serves to expand the role of the bodhrán and to transcend its acoustic limitations.

Robert Daly, an American bodhrán player and instructor, demonstrated a new concept in bodhrán playing that ventures toward the role of multipercussionist. He uses synthesizer drum pedals that produce a drum kit kick bass drum sound and a snare drum sound. He plays simple bass and snare drum patterns while playing the bodhrán. He also has attached a wireless pick-up microphone inside the bodhrán rim. He runs the audio from this microphone into effects units, which can drastically alter the sound of his bodhrán. Daly pairs the bodhrán with synthesizer drum pedals as opposed to performing these rhythms on a drum kit due to the bodhrán's strong associative ties to Irish traditional music and its status as an authentic native

Irish instrument. Daly's technological experimentation was an attempt to increase the musical possibilities of the bodhrán and to incorporate different percussive timbres into his performances.

Rónán Ó Snodaigh's desire to broaden the bodhrán's timbral spectrum has resulted in filtering the mic'd bodhrán's sound through electronic devices. He explained, "I am trying to get more effects on the bodhrán. There's a fella who made a wah-wah pedal for me. Fattened the amplitude. I have a tremolo pedal as well. I am excited getting into electronics. I have been playing a Korg wave drum. I got it triggered ten to fifteen years ago to trigger a drum set, while I was playing the bodhrán with a small EQ pickup. I have a splitter system. Any time I can do something different with the bodhrán, I'm excited." Ó Snodaigh's solo and ensemble performance on the Korg wave drum (a digital drum synthesizer with a responsive, synthetic drumhead) grants him access to a large sound bank of percussion instruments. Turning the drum on its side, Ó Snodaigh strikes the drumhead with his tipper just like a bodhrán. He has incorporated several of the Korg's world percussion synth patches into his percussive work with Kíla and his own solo work.

Delving deeper into the sounds of the mic'd bodhrán, Ó Snodaigh has recorded an album entitled *Epic Bodhrán*. It consists of bodhrán drum loops intended for music producers to sample. This recording marks a progressive step toward greater familiarity and sonic availability for the drum and offers a plethora of musical possibilities for electronically inclined musicians.

Further exploring the electronic technological possibilities of the bodhrán, a group of computer researchers at the University of Limerick

Rónán Ó Snodaigh playing a wave drum. (Dublin, Ireland. Courtesy of Rónán Ó Snodaigh, 2018)

developed a virtual bodhrán called the "vodhran." This is a musical interface that serves an alternative gestural controller. A Polhemus Fastrak sensory device for tracking user movements was coupled with PureData for Linnux computer software that mapped certain gestures and assigned specific gestures with assigned sounds. By placing a sensor on the tipper and tracking a player's performance gestures, the vodhran serves as an expressive sound object that relies on a player's performance gestures as a means of producing a set of assigned sounds (Marshall, Rath, and Moynihan 2002, 1–2). This technological abstraction allows bodhrán players to perform musical patterns through gesture alone without needing a physical drum.

Four

THE REPERTORY

———————

The following annotated list includes academic publications, scores, instructional materials, film and television episodes, literary fiction, online resources, and seminal recordings that feature the bodhrán. Sources are provided that offer insight into the developing nature of bodhrán performance practices. The texts and recordings enclosed offer particular knowledge regarding drum techniques, sound production, musical roles, drum pedagogy, orchestration, organological history, and influential performers spanning the drum's recent rise in popularity from the 1950s to present.

The academic publications included are limited in number due to the dearth of research regarding the bodhrán. Ethnomusicological texts, folklore articles, and percussion articles are included based upon the history and stylistic developments described by the relevant authors.

The scores are primarily from motion pictures where the bodhrán was included. A much smaller number of western art music scores are provided where composers have written explicitly for the bodhrán in a chamber ensemble or orchestral context.

The recordings presented here are by necessity highly selective. Their inclusion is based on their high standard of instrumental mastery, stylistic distinctions, instrumental technical developments, the demonstrated musical role of the drum, and overall musicality. Preference is given to the highest quality recordings from a diverse group of bodhrán performers. Multiple recordings from individuals or groups are presented based on their differing musical output, distinction in musical presentation, and significant, percussive influence on bodhrán players.

INSTRUCTIONAL MATERIALS

Absolute Beginners: Bodhrán. 2000. DVD. Waltons.

Conor Long offers a bodhrán instructional video with an accompanying book and CD for novices. Rudimentary instrumental techniques and accompaniment patterns are explained and demonstrated with the expectation that the student will start and stop the video to practice.

Beginner Bodhrán Instruction. 2013. DVD. Steve Doyle Studios.

John McBride instructs beginning bodhrán players, offering information on the history of bodhrán, seisún protocol, bodhrán models and tippers, and accompaniment patterns using the double-ended tipper style for standard reels, jigs, and slip jigs.

Bodhrán & Bones. 1994. Alfred.

Mel Mercier provides a comprehensive instructional video introducing bodhrán accompaniment techniques for traditional tune forms. Similarly, Mercier demonstrates different bones techniques. Video performances show Mercier accompanying flautist Séamus Egan.

Bodhrán, Bones & Spoons. 2000. Hal Leonard.

The Bodhrán. 2005. Music Sales.

Tommy Hayes leads an exhaustive instructional video exploring a wide variety of conventional and experimental bodhrán techniques and accompaniment strategies. He also demonstrates spoons and bones techniques. Hayes includes his own approach to these instruments, demonstrated through multiple performances.

Bodhrán Soup. 2011. Musify Media.

Eamon Murray has created an instructional video that covers recent modern developments in bodhrán accompaniment. Murray focuses on single-ended tipper style while demonstrating techniques and rhythmic patterns that are influenced by nontraditional music of the world.

Bodhrán-Tutorial mit Guido Plueschke: Hit the Goat. 2013. DVD. Liekedeler Musikproduktionen.

This is the first German instruction DVD for beginning students of the bodhrán.

Boyd, Alison. 2011. *Bodhran Practice.* CD. Privately published.

This beginner instructional CD features Alison Boyd explaining and performing Irish traditional tune form such as the reel, jig, and hornpipe. It contains slow sets of tunes for beginners to play along with.

Daly, Robert. 2007. *The Bodhrán: An Irish Drum.* Albany: Celtic Percussion.

Robert Daly wrote a bodhrán instructional book that uses snare drum exercise patterns to be applied to the bodhrán. He uses a system in which western music notation is combined with arrows to indicate stick direction as well as colored and open circles to indicate hand placement. These snare drum patterns are used as different exercises to apply to reels and jig patterns. The notation book also contains bodhrán drum patterns in unusual time signatures such as 7/8 and 5/4.

Driver, Nicholas. 1988. *Nicholas Driver's Bodhran and Bones Tutor.* Hampshire,
UK: Hobgoblin Books.
This instructional textbook explains the basics techniques of bodhrán and
bones playing with short histories and maintenance information for both
instruments.

Grady, Mance. 1995. *Playing the Irish Drum: Getting Started.* DVD. Privately
published.
Bodhrán maker and performer Mance Grady demonstrates the fundamentals
of playing the bodhrán.

Hannigan, Steáfán. 1991. *The Bodhrán Book.* Cork: Ossian.
Hannigan has written an educational text for beginners. It contains western
music notation and utilizes arrows to show direction and reel patterns. The
double-ended tipper style is solely employed.

Houlihan, Peter. 2007. *The Irish Drum: An Bodhrán.* West Yorkshire:
Dave Mallinson.
Text intended for beginner bodhrán players. Peter Houlihan provides jig,
reel, hornpipe, slides, polka, march, and slip jig rhythmic patterns. Arrows
indicating tipper-striking direction, mnemonic rhythmic devices and
related tune notation are provided. Musical examples are provided on an
accompanying CD.

How to Play the Bodhrán. 2007. DVD. Lark in the Morning.
Chris Caswell provides an introductory instructional video that explains
the basic playing techniques for the bodhrán, bones, spoons, and Scottish
snare drum.

Irish Heartbeat: A Bodhrán Tutorial by Ray Gallen. 2006. DVD. Doonaree.
Intended for beginning students. Ray Gallen introduces basic bodhrán
accompaniment patterns for jigs, reels, and polkas.

Learn to Play the Irish Bodhrán Drum with Michael Vignoles. 2006. DVD. Vignoles
Bodhran Drums.
Bodhrán maker Michael Vignoles provides bodhrán accompaniment patterns
and strategies for beginning and intermediate students.

Mad For Trad. 2001. CD-ROM. Cork: Mad For Trad.
Frank Torpey provides basic and advanced bodhrán accompaniment for jig.

Masterclass Celtic Beat: Traditional Music from Ireland. 1998. CD. Outlet
Recording.
Directed toward beginner and intermediate students, Ray Gallen
demonstrates how to play with reels, jigs, hornpipes, polkas, and slides.

Murphy, Martin. 1997. *The International Bodhran Book.* Rathdrum, ID: John
Ellison.
This multilingual, instructional text provides instructions and diagrams for
novice bodhrán students.

O'Brien, Fergal. 2017. *Grade 2 Bodhrán Tutor & CD.* Privately published.
This instructional text provides a bodhrán curriculum aligned with the
London College of Music's Irish traditional music syllabus and examination.

The text contains up/down arrows, music notation of Irish tune melodies (reels, jigs, barn dances, slip jigs, polkas, march, hornpipe, mazurka) and bodhrán accompanying rhythms, and different lyrics that match the different tune's rhythmic patterns.

Ó Súilleabháin, Mícheál. 1984. *The Bodhrán: An Easy to Learn Method for the Complete Beginner Showing the Different Regional Styles and Techniques.* Dublin: Waltons.

Centered around beginner bodhrán instruction, the text includes a brief history of the bodhrán, music notation of rhythmic patterns with up and down accents for Irish traditional tune forms, tipper grips and styles, and modern drum techniques and rhythmic ornamentations.

Paddy League. 2004. *An Gabhairín Binn: A Bodhrán Tutor.* Bloomington, IN: Paddy League.

This instructional text is for beginning and intermediate students. It contains musical notation of Irish traditional tune forms. The book comes with an accompanying CD with tunes played at normal and half speed with featuring Grey Larsen on tin whistle and Paddy League on bodhrán.

Smith, Robin M. 1993. *Power Bodhran Techniques: The New Approach to the Celtic Drum.* West Melbourne, FL: Mid-East.

This instructional text is intended for beginner bodhrán students. It provides basic rhythmic accompaniment for Irish traditional tune forms.

Stone, Mark. 2005. *The Bodhran.* CD Baby.

Mark Stone has recorded an instructional CD with recorded tracks of reels jigs, slip jigs, hornpipes, slides, and polkas with variations. It is intended for beginner and intermediate students to practice with.

Sullivan, Tony. 2006. *Learn to Play the Bodhran.* Manchester: Halshaw Music.

This instructional text provides bodhrán accompaniment for Irish jigs, reels, polkas, and hornpipes. The CD provides twenty-one practice tunes intended for beginning students. Steáfán Hannigan provides bodhrán demonstrations, playing techniques, western notation of reels and jigs, and a discussion of conceptual approaches. The DVD is accompanied by a detailed booklet containing descriptions of musical forms such as the reel or jig as well as notated examples of specific rhythmic patterns.

Woods, Bill. 2009. *Bodhran: The Basics.* Fenton, MO: Mel Bay.

This instruction book and CD is organized for the beginning bodhrán player. Along with photographs, text, and audio examples, basic techniques covering accompaniment patterns for reels and jigs using rests, accents, and rolls are included. The CD features tunes recorded at different tempos for student practice.

———. 2011. *Bodhran: Beyond the Basics.* Fenton, MO: Mel Bay.

Suited for intermediate bodhrán players, the instructional text and CD contain exercises and solos for jig, reels, waltzes, and slip jigs. Along with the exercises and solos, different time signatures, syncopation, speed control, pitch and timbral manipulation, and dexterity are covered.

ACADEMIC PUBLICATIONS

Carver, Bruce. 2012. "Bones and Bodhran: Beyond Tradition." *Percussive Notes* 50 (5): 78–80.
This brief article discusses the different timbral opportunities for percussive arrangement of the bodhrán and bones.

Forsthoff, K., and Andy Kruspe. 2013. "The Irish Bodhrán in Context: Celebrating the Evolutions of a Modern Tradition." *Percussive Notes* 51 (5): 20–22.
This percussive arts society article succinctly explains is the history of the bodhrán and its rapid development as a percussive accompaniment instrument.

Kearns, Malachy. 1996. *Wallup: Humour and Lore of Bodhrán Making.* Connemara: Roundstone Music Instruments.
This anecdotal text discusses the challenges involved in making a suitable bodhrán.

McCauley, Jacob. 2011. "The Bodhrán Demystified." *DRUM! Magazine*, 185, 69–73.
McCauley offers a brief overview of performance techniques such as tone control and tipper playing styles.

———. 2013. "The Contemporary Bodhrán Player." *Living Tradition*, January, 54–56.
This brief article explains bodhrán tuning systems, different tippers, and skin muting.

McCrickard, Janet E. 1987. *The Bodhrán: The Background to the Traditional Irish Drum.* Glastonbury: Fieldfare Art and Design.
McCrickard draws upon an eclectic range of secondary sources in an attempt to explain the origins and early cultural traditions associated with bodhrán. The text's historical research ranges from speculative to evidence-based due its wide academic breadth.

Morrison, Scott. 2011. "The History of the Bodhrán: Ireland's 'Native Drum.'" *Percussive Notes* 49 (3): 38–41.
Morrison provides a brief history of the origins and organological development of the bodhrán.

Ó Bharáin, Liam. 2007. "Bodhrán – Its Origin, Meaning, and History." *Treoir* 39 (4): 50–56.

———. 2008. "Bodhrán – Its Recent History: Making and Playing the Bodhrán." *Treoir* 40 (1): 47–52.

———. 2008. "Bodhrán – Its Recent History: Making and Playing the Bodhrán." *Treoir* 40 (2): 49–56.
This three-part article offers a comprehensive historiography of the bodhrán.

O'Mahoney, Terry. 1999. "The Irish Bodhrán." *Percussive Notes* 7 (2): 34–40.
O'Mahoney provides a brief history of the drum, playing styles and performance tips, and design and maintenance observations.

Ó Súilleabháin, Mícheál. 1974. "The Bodhrán." *Treoir* 6, 4–5.
Ó Súilleabháin gives a brief history of the drum and related performance practices.

Schiller, Rina. 2001. *The Lambeg and the Bodhrán*. Belfast: Institute of Irish Studies, Queen's University.
This comparative, ethnomusicological text explores drum construction, societal drum use, performance practices, and histories of both the lambeg and bodhrán.

Such, David G. 1985. "The Bodhrán: The Black Sheep in the Family of Traditional Irish Musical Instruments." *Galpin Society Journal* 38, 9–19.
Such offers a detailed history of the drum, bodhrán making, and cultural perceptions of the role of the drum and performer.

Vallely, Fintan, ed. 1999. "Bodhrán." In *The Companion to Irish Traditional Music*. Cork: Cork University Press.
This comprehensive, referential text for Irish traditional music offers a lengthy entry explaining the historical development of the bodhrán.

WEBSITES

Bell, Matthew. The Contemporary Bodhrán, accessed April 9, 2017. contemporarybodhran.com.
Matthew Bell offers a comprehensive instructional course (video, music notation, audio examples) on how to play the bodhrán.

Bodhrán, accessed April 9, 2017. www.bodojo.com.
This online community forum is where contributors share information regarding the bodhrán. There is a vast selection of threads pertaining to the bodhrán regarding makers, performers, recordings, techniques, humor, history, upcoming concerts, and educational resources. This forum has recently moved to the bodojo group on facebook as a continuation of the bodojo website and online community.

Bodhrán, accessed April 9, 2017. https://thesession.org/.
The session is an online community forum where contributors share information regarding topics pertinent to Irish traditional music. There is vast selection of threads pertaining to the bodhrán regarding makers, performers, recordings, techniques, humor, history and educational resources. Bodhrán, accessed February 21, 2018. https://comhaltas.ie/.
Comhaltas Ceoltóirí Éireann is a nonprofit cultural organization focused on the preservation and promotion of Irish traditional music. This website offers countless video clips, photos, and audio clips of bodhrán music making.

Bodhrán, accessed February 21, 2018. https://www.itma.ie/.
The Irish Traditional Music Archive located in Dublin offers an online digital library with innumerable bodhrán-based sound recordings, books, videos, manuscripts, and images.

Bodhrán, accessed April 9, 2017. https://www.oaim.ie/.

The Online Academy of Irish Music provides video instruction for beginner to advanced students for a range of instruments including the bodhrán. Brian Fleming and Jim Higgins demonstrate a variety of techniques spaced across multiple video selections.

Chastain, Blayne. Online Bodhrán Lessons, accessed April 9, 2017. https://www .blaynechastain.com/i-teach/.

Blayne Chastain offers a course centered around instructional videos and an accompanying PDF that demonstrates basic instrumental techniques using a double-ended tipper style.

Ó Snodaigh, Rónán. Bodhrán Classes 1–24, accessed April 9, 2017. https://www .youtube.com/playlist?list=PLs9gZLtX3Dv9Vr8pHxS95OrYfPST1RcbT.

Ó Snodaigh provides a 24-class video instruction series that explores standard and experimental bodhrán playing techniques.

Stewart, Michelle. Bodhrán Expert, accessed April 9, 2017. Bodhranexpert.com.

Stewart has created a slew of online instructional videos covering a range of beginner, intermediate, and advanced topics from tipper selection to playing in odd meters (e.g., 7/4 time signature).

SOUNDTRACKS

Afro Celt Sound System. 1996. "Dark Moon, High Tide." *Gangs of New York.* Universal.

Afro Celt Sound System provides one composition to the *Gangs of New York* soundtrack featuring James McNally on bodhrán.

Burwell, Carter. 1995. *Rob Roy.* Virgin.

Arranged by Carter Burwell, the Chieftains contributes one selection, arranged by Michael Turbridy, entitled "Sullivan's March," featuring Kevin Conneff on bodhrán for the soundtrack. Tommy Hayes and Marc Duff of Capercaillie provide bodhrán accompaniment on separate tracks.

The Chieftains. 1976. *Barry Lyndon.* Warner Bros UK.

Paddy Moloney's score contributes two selections with bodhrán entitled "Piper's Maggot Jig" and "Tin Whistles" featuring Peadar Mercier on bodhrán.

——. 1984. *The Grey Fox.* DRG.

Paddy Moloney's score contributes one selection entitled "The Main Theme" featuring Kevin Conneff on bodhrán.

——. 1990. *Treasure Island.* TNT.

Paddy Moloney's score is performed by the Chieftains featuring Kevin Conneff on bodhrán.

——. 1991. *Ireland Moving.* RCA.

Paddy Moloney's score contributes one selection entitled "Train Sequence" featuring Kevin Conneff on bodhrán.

Coulais, Bruce, and Kíla. 2009. *The Secret of Kells*. Kíla Records.
> Coulais's score was written in collaboration with the Irish folk rock band Kíla. The soundtrack features Rónán Ó Snodaigh on bodhrán.

———. 2014. *Song of the Sea*. Decca Records.
> Coulais's score was written in collaboration with the Irish folk rock band Kíla. The soundtrack features Rónán Ó Snodaigh on bodhrán.

Daring, Mason. 1994. *The Secret of Roan Inish*. Jones Entertainment Group.
> Daring's score includes occasional bodhrán accompaniment, performed by Mel Mercier.

Doyle, Patrick. 2012. *Brave*. Walt Disney.
> Doyle's musical score features bodhrán accompaniment by Jim Sutherland.

Egan, Séamus. 1995. *The Brothers McMullen*. Fox Searchlight Pictures.
> Having arranged the film score, Séamus Egan performs on flute and bodhrán with Tommy Hayes offering additional bodhrán accompaniment for this soundtrack.

Fenton, George. 2006. *The Wind That Shakes the Barley*. Kronos Records.
> Fenton's film score features brief bodhrán orchestration.

Forman, Steve. 2006. *Don't Wait Up*. Steve Forman.
> Forman composed this piece in order to incorporate the bodhrán in chamber ensembles. This score features clarinet, bassoon, cello, and bodhrán.

———. 2008. *The Clydean Coronaries*. Steve Forman.
> Forman's chamber ensemble composition features the constant drive of bodhrán and Scottish highland pipes while the brass orchestration complements the aforementioned instruments.

———. 2009. *Hameward Bend*. Steve Forman.
> Written for full orchestra, this composition strongly features Northumbrian border pipes and bodhráns.

Horner, James. 1995. *Braveheart*. London Classics.
> Horner's movie score features bodhrán, performed by Mike Taylor.

———. 1997. *Titanic*. Masterworks.
> The bodhrán is included in this James Horner film score, performed by Stephen Wehmeyer of Gaelic Storm.

Kamen, Michael. 1995. *Circle of Friends*. Warner Bros.
> Michael Kamen's score contributes two selections performed by the Chieftains: an air and a jig entitled "Dublin." The jig features Kevin Conneff on bodhrán.

McCreary, Bear. 2014. *Black Sails*. Starz.
> Composer Bear McCreary's score features the rhythmic duo of Los Angeles session percussionists Bruce Carver (bodhrán) and Brad Dutz (bones). Carver and Dutz creatively perform in an improvisatory manner in relation to a score that includes unusual time signatures (e.g., 7/4), European folk instruments (e.g., hurdy gurdy), and orchestral instruments in a non-Irish traditional context.

Ó Riada, Seán. 1962. *Playboy of the Western World*. Gael Linn Records.
Seán Ó Riada and Ceoltorí Cualann provide the film score featuring Seán Ó Riada on bodhrán.

Whelan, Bill. 1994. *Riverdance*. Riverdance.
Whelan's score features the bodhrán sporadically throughout the dance performance. Tommy Hayes was the original bodhrán performer for the show.

Williams, John. 1992. *Far and Away*. MCA.
William's score features performances by the Chieftains with Kevin Conneff on bodhrán.

RECORDINGS

Altan. 2002. *The Blue Idol*. Narada.
Features the bodhrán accompaniment of guest artist Jim Higgins on a selection of jigs, reels, and songs in Irish Gaelic and English.

An Tara. 2015. *The Space Between*. Independent Release.
This duet recording features Matthew Noone on the sarod, a twenty-three-string North Indian lute, and Tommy Hayes on bodhrán, bones, spoons, marimba, bells, mbira, jaw harp, silk worm cocoons, and goat toenails. The recording contains original compositions exploring aspects of Irish traditional music, Indian classical music, and improvisation. Hayes performs on the bodhrán using a tipper and two-hand doumbek-inspired hand striking.

Arcady. 1992. *After the Ball*. Shanachie Records.
Founding group member Johnny "Ringo" McDonagh provides bodhrán, bones, and triangle accompaniment for an assortment of Irish jigs, reels, and barn dances as well as Breton reels.

———. 1995. *Many Happy Returns*. Shanachie Records.
McDonagh offers bodhrán, bones, and triangle accompaniment to a variety of Irish traditional tunes.

Beoga. 2005. *A Lovely Madness*. Compass Records.
The progressive bodhrán accompaniment of founding member Eamon Murray is featured on this recording as he navigates complex, cosmopolitan arrangements of jigs, reels, and polkas.

———. 2007. *Mischief*. Compass Records.
The bodhrán playing of Eamon Murray weaves through nontraditional arrangements and rhythms. His accompaniment is complemented by assorted percussion (shakers and drum kit).

———. 2009. *The Incident*. Compass Records.
Eamon Murray's bodhrán accompaniment is complemented by shaker percussion on eclectic arrangements of reels, jigs, a waltz, and nontraditional song covers.

——. 2011. *How to Tune a Fish*. Compass Records.

Eamon Murray plays bodhrán, shaker, and snare while accompanying group-written compositions of reels, jigs, slides, and songs that draw upon a wealth of nontraditional musical influences.

——. 2016. *Before We Changed Our Mind*. Compass Records.

Eamon Murray provides progressive, drum-kit inspired rhythmic accompaniment on the bodhrán for group-penned compositions.

Bergin, Mary. 1979. *Feadoga Stain*. Gael Linn.

Johnny McDonagh accompanies the rapid tin whistling of Mary Bergin on bodhrán and bones.

The Boys of the Lough. 1973. *The Boys of the Lough*. Trailer.

Robin Morton performs open, double-ended tipper-styled bodhrán accompaniment for reels, jigs, and songs.

Bradley, Harry. 1999. *Bad Turns & Horse-Shoe Bends*. Outlet Records.

Seamus O'Kane offers subtle bodhrán accompaniment for the Irish traditional flute playing of Harry Bradley.

The Breeze from Erin: Irish Folk Music on Wind Instruments. 1969. Topic Records.

This compilation of Irish traditional wind instrumentalists features a rare recording of Seamus Tansey's hand-struck bodhrán (listed as tambourine) accompaniment on a set of reels: "Bonny Kate/ Jenny's Chickens."

Buille. 2009. *2*. Crow Valley Music.

This eclectic recording features Brian Morrissey's bodhrán accompaniment for Niall Vallely's tunes, drawing upon Irish traditional music, jazz, and western art music.

——. 2015. *Beo*. Crow Valley Music.

Bully's Acre. 2014. *The Twelve Pins*. Big Beat Music.

Robbie Harris provides bodhrán accompaniment that explores Irish traditional music with Iberian musical influences.

Cara. 2016. *Yet We Sing*. Artes Records.

Rolf Wagels gives bodhrán accompaniment in a modern ensemble format featuring group-penned tunes and songs.

Celtic Thunder. 1988. *The Light of Other Days*. Green Linnet.

This Irish American band performs traditional Irish songs, tunes, and original compositions. The album contains bodhrán accompaniment by Jessie Winch featuring a bodhrán solo entitled "The Flaming Shillelagh."

Chieftains. 1963. *1*. Island Records.

This initial recording features the unmuted bodhrán playing of David Fallon

——. 1969. *2*. Claddagh Records.

This second recording introduces the bodhrán playing of Peadar Mercier.

——. 1971. *3*. Claddagh Records.

——. 1973. *4*. Claddagh Records.

——. 1975. *5*. Claddagh Records.

——. 1976. *Bonaparte's Retreat*. Claddagh Records.

Kevin Conneff replaces Peadar Mercier on bodhrán. Additional percussion credits are given to Paddy Moloney and Seán Potts. Conneff would become a full member of the Chieftains and remains as their current bodhrán performer.

Cían. 1999. *Three Shouts from a Hill*. Cían Records.
Damien Quinn offers lively bodhrán accompaniment in an ensemble format for Irish traditional tunes.

Comas. 2005. *Comas*. Mad River Records.
Jackie Moran is featured on bodhrán, bones, hand drum, and cymbals playing an assortment of jigs, reels, polkas, a hornpipe, a waltz, and a song.

Cooley, Joe. 1975. *Cooley*. Gael-Linn.
Jack Cooley provides unmuted, rhythmic accompaniment on a bodhrán with jingles using a hand-striking technique.

Danú. 2000. *Think before You Think*. Shanachie Records.
Features the tapping, rhythmic bodhrán accompaniment of Donnchadh Gough in a modern Irish traditional music ensemble.

——. 2002. *All Things Considered*. Shanachie Records.

——. 2004. *Up in the Air*. Shanachie Records.

——. 2005. *When All Is Said and Done*. Shanachie Records.

Datta, Soumik, and City of London Sinfonia. 2018. *King of Ghosts*. Globe Music.
Sarod virtuoso Soumik Datta performs with the City of London Sinfonia to provide an original score for the 1968 film *King of Ghosts*. Cormac Byrne performs on his Blackwell Original Drums Talking Bodhrán and aluminum sliding sound bar to provide tabla-inspired percussive accompaniment.

Davey, Junior. 2005. *A Sound Skin*. Coleman Heritage Center.
Accompanying on bones and bodhrán, Junior Davey performs Irish traditional music in an ensemble format.

Davies, Peter Maxwell. 2012. *Symphony No. 3 / Cross Lane Fair*. BBC Philharmonic, *Maxwell Davies*. Naxos Records.
Cross Lane Fair is a western art music composition, scored for Northumbrian pipes, bodhrán (performed by Rob Lea), and chamber orchestra, inspired by the memories of a fairground that Davies visited as a child.

Dé Danann. 1977. *Selected Jigs, Reels & Songs*. Decca Records.
This virtuosic Irish traditional music ensemble is accompanied on hand-muted bodhrán by Johnny McDonagh. This recording includes an early bodhrán solo.

De Dannan. 1991. *Hibernian Rhapsody*. Shanachie Records.
Colm Murphy gives this famous ensemble his rapid fire, treble bodhrán accompaniment on Irish traditional music and popular music arrangements.

De Dannan. 2012. *Jigs, Reels & Rock 'n' Roll*. Tara Records.
As the album title suggests, a variety of Irish traditional music and popular music is accompanied by bodhrán player Eric Cunningham.

Dervish. 2000. *Midsummer's Night*. Alliance.
This ensemble recording occasionally features the soft patter of Cathy Jordan's bodhrán accompaniment.

Dutz, Brad, and Bruce Carver. 2012. *Bones and Bodhrán: Beyond Tradition*. Leaky Spleen.

Famed for their studio session work for soundtracks, Brad Dutz (bones) and Bruce Carver (bodhrán) offer an interactive, improvisatory percussive duet that spans a variety of musical genres.

Easy Club. 1985. *Chance or Design*. Rel Records.

Featuring Scottish tunes and songs blended with swing musical sensibilities, Jim Sutherland provides bodhrán accompaniment using wooden tipper and brush tipper. This album contains one of the earliest recorded bodhrán solos.

Flook. 2000. *Flatfish*. Flatfish Records.

This recording features the highly influential, virtuosic bodhrán playing of John Joe Kelly in a progressive ensemble format performing group-penned tunes.

——. 2002. *Rubai*. Flatfish Records.

——. 2005. *Haven*. Flatfish Records.

Folan, Declan, and Junior Davey. 1995. *Skin and Bow*. Sound Records.

Bodhrán pedagogue and performer Junior Davey expertly provides modern percussive accompaniment to the melodic fiddle playing of Declan Folan.

Four Men and a Dog. 1991. *Barking Mad*. Green Linnet Records.

Gino Lupari provides driving bodhrán accompaniment for Irish traditional tunes and songs.

——. 1994. *Shifting Gravel*. Green Linnet.

——. 1995. *Dr. A's Secret Melodies*. Transatlantic Records.

——. 1996. *Long Roads*. Transatlantic Records.

——. 2002. *Maybe Tonight*. Hook.

——. 2007. *Wallop the Spot*. Hook.

FourWinds. 2015. *FourWinds*. Independent Release.

Robbie Walsh offers bodhrán accompaniment for a variety of Irish traditional tunes and songs.

Goitse. 2014. *Transformed*. Goitse.

Colm Phelan provides high-energy, cosmopolitan bodhrán accompaniment in an ensemble format performing group-penned tunes.

——. 2014. *Tall Tales & Misadventures*. Goitse.

——. 2016. *Inspired by Chance*. Goitse.

Hayes, Tommy. 1991. *An Rás*. Mulligan Records.

Tommy Hayes provides rhythmic accompaniment on a wide variety of percussion instruments with a particular focus on hand-struck frame drums (e.g. daf, tar, doumbek) and the bodhrán. Irish, Scottish, and jazz music are explored in this recording. This is one of the first solo albums released by an Irish bodhrán player/percussionist.

——. 1997. *A Room in the North*. Hanna Music.

Hayes's second album features him on bodhrán using tipper and hand-striking along with assorted percussion. The recording also includes Julia

Haines (harp), Ronan Brown (flutes), Kenneth Edge (saxophone), and
Hayes's aunt, Meta Costelloe.

Hayes, Tommy, and Ian Leslie. 2009. *Almost Home*. Claddagh Records.
This eclectic recording documents the collaboration between Ian Leslie
(saxophonist) and Tommy Hayes (percussionist), resulting in original
compositions and arrangements that blend reverbed singing and Irish
traditional instruments with percussion, woodwinds, strings, and brass.

Hussain, Zakir. 2015. *Distant Kin*. Moment Records.
Tabla virtuoso Zakir Hussain collaborates with Irish and Scottish musicians
to explore blended arrangements of Indian and Celtic music. John Joe Kelly
is featured on bodhrán throughout the live album and performs an extensive
drum solo on "Trinkamp/Tajir."

Kasír. 2010. *Chilling on a Sunday*. GO Danish Folk Music.
Oisín Walsh provides progressive bodhrán accompaniment for this Danish
trio performing new compositions inspired by Irish traditional music.

Kelly, Liam, and Philip Duffy. 2016. *Sets in Stone*. Independent Release.
This recording of flautist Liam Kelly (Dervish) and fiddler Philip Duffy
includes bodhrán accompaniment by John Joe Kelly.

Kíla. 1999. *Tóg É Go Bog É*. Green Linnet.
Rónán Ó Snodaigh provides vocals and accompanies the Irish folk rock
group on bodhrán, hand drums, shakers, and assorted percussion.

Larsen, Grey, and Paddy League. 2001. *The Green House*. CD Baby.
The duet recording features the progressive, pitch-sliding bodhrán playing of
Paddy League.

Lyons, Neill. 2009. *Skins and Sins*. CD Baby.
This recording by bodhrán player Neill Lyons features an assortment of guest
melody players as they perform Irish traditional dance music. A fine bodhrán
solo is provided as well.

Mithril. 2007. *The Return Home*. CD Baby.
With progressive arrangements of Breton, Macedonian, and Irish traditional
music, Andy Kruspe offers drum-kit inspired bodhrán accompaniment.

Moore, Christy. 1991. *Smoke and Strong Whiskey*. Sony.
While Moore's singing and guitar playing dominate this recording, his hand-
striking bodhrán accompaniment can be heard throughout, most notably in
Aisling and *Green Island*.

Mórga. 2009. *Mórga*. Pug Records.
Dominic Keogh performs on flute and bodhrán on an assortment of Irish
traditional tunes.

Morrison, Tom, and John Reynolds. 1927. *Columbia 33210-F,* 78 rpm.
John Reynolds gives bodhrán accompaniment to Galway flute player Tom
Morrison on the first known recording of the bodhrán.

——. 1927. *Columbia 33308-F,* 78 rpm.

——. 1927. *Columbia 33247-F,* 78 rpm.

——. 1927. *Columbia 33260-F,* 78 rpm.

———. 1928. *Columbia 33293-F*, 78 rpm.

The Mountain Road: A Compilation of Tunes Popular in South Sligo. Coleman Heritage Center.

This compilation recording features the South Sligo, open, hand-struck bodhrán accompaniment of Ted McGowan.

Moving Cloud. 2005. *Sweet Nyaa.* GO Danish Folk Music.

Svend Kjeldsen accompanies Irish traditional tunes on bodhrán. The album is produced by Dónal Lunny. The bodhrán is featured prominently in the album's overall mix.

Murphy, Colm. 1996. *An Bodhrán.* Gael-Linn.

Colm Murphy provides light, fluid bodhrán accompaniment using a double-ended tipper for a variety of jigs, reels, hornpipes, slides, and polkas.

Nomos. 1995. *I'm Not Afraid Anymore.* Green Linnet Records.

Frank Torpey provide steady, driving bodhrán accompaniment for Irish traditional tunes. Assorted hand drums and percussion are included.

———. 1997. *Set You Free.* Green Linnet Records.

Ó Maonlaí, Liam. 2005. *Rian.* Rian Records.

Ó Maonlaí's bodhrán playing provides a rhythmic counterpoint to his singing in this solo recording.

Ó Murchú, Marcas. 2006. *Turas Ceoil.* Cló Iar-Chonnacht.

Marcas Ó Murchú and guest artists are accompanied on bodhrán by Seamus O'Kane on a variety of jigs, reels, and polkas.

Ó Riada, Seán. 1969. *Ó Riada Sa Gaiety.* Gael Linn.

Recorded live at the Gaiety Theater in Dublin. Seán Ó Riada's Ceoltóirí Chualann provides an energetic ensemble performance featuring the unmuted, rhythmic bodhrán playing of Peadar Mercier.

Ó Snodaigh, Rónán. 2004. *Tonnta Ro.* Kíla Records.

This solo album features vocal, guitar, and percussion (bodhrán, shakers, jingles, hand drums) performances by Rónán Ó Snodaigh.

Ó Snodaigh, Rónán. 2015. *Epic Bodhrán.* Squirky Music.

Ó Snodaigh has recorded an album of bodhrán drum loops intended for music producers to sample.

O'Neill, Martin. 2012. *In Session.* Martin O'Neill.

Martin O'Neill accompanies guest artists performing musical styles ranging from Irish traditional music to Scottish bagpiping to jazz.

O'Suilleabhain, Micheal. 1987. *Dolphin's Way.* Virgin Venture.

Mel Mercier offers bodhrán and bones accompaniment for Micheal O'Suilleabhain's progressive arrangements of Irish traditional tunes.

Phelan, Colm. 2012. *Full Circle.* Colm Phelan.

This solo recording features Colm Phelan accompanying a host of guest artists on bodhrán, frequently in a duet format.

Planxty. 1973. *Planxty.* Shanachie.

Christy Moore offers hand-struck bodhrán accompaniment on a relatively unmuted drum skin.

——. 1973. *Well below the Valley*. Shanachie.

Christy Moore offers hand-struck bodhrán accompaniment on a set of reels and slip jigs.

——. 1974. *Cold Blow and the Rainy Night*. Shanachie.

This recording features the hand-struck bodhrán accompaniment of Christy Moore and Dónal Lunny.

——. 1979. *After the Break*. Tara Records.

Christy Moore accompanies a set of jigs and reels. This recording is noteworthy for Moore's bodhrán accompaniment of a Bulgarian folk tune, *Smeceno Horo*, in 9/16 meter.

Plüschke, Guido, and Rolf Wagels. 2011. *Bodhrán Insight*. Liekedeler Musikproduktionen.

This recording seeks to demonstrate the musical versatility of the bodhrán.

Puck Fair. 1987. *Fair Play*. Windham Hill Records.

The trio of Brian Dunning, Mícheál Ó Domhnaill, and Tommy Hayes perform cosmopolitan arrangements that seamlessly blend jazz, Celtic music, and contemporary influences. The virtuosic bodhrán playing of Tommy Hayes is prominently featured.

Pure Bodhrán: The Definitive Collection. 2005. Big Beat Music.

This compilation provides a multitude of professional bodhrán players, offering a track per drummer. This recording is a wonderful introduction to various bodhrán performance styles.

Seán Ó Sé le Seán Ó Riada, with Ceoltóirí Chualann. 2010. *An Poc Ar Buile Agus Amhráin Eile*. Independent Records.

This rerelease of an early 1960s recording features Seán Ó Sé's singing accompanied by Ceoltóirí Chualann. Seán Ó Riada performs on bodhrán and harpsichord.

Shannon, Garry, and Orfhlaith Ní Bhriain. 1989. *Lose the Head*. A Brick Missing Music Records.

Mossie Griffin deftly accompanies jigs, reels, hornpipes, and songs on bodhrán.

Smith, Ivan. 2003. *Champions of Ireland — Bodhrán*. Connoisseur Records.

This recording features All Ireland bodhrán champion Ivan Smith accompanying an assortment of reels, jigs, slides, and slow airs. There is a bodhrán solo included as well.

Stockton's Wing. 1978. *Stockton's Wing*. Tara Music.

Tommy Hayes provides accompaniment on bodhrán and jaw harp for Irish traditional jigs, reels, slip jig, songs, and a mazurka.

Téada. 2003. *Téada*. Green Linnet Records.

Tristan Rosenstock provides bodhrán accompaniment for Irish traditional tunes and songs.

——. 2004. *Give Us a Penny and Let Us Be Gone*. Green Linnet Records.

——. 2006. *Inné Amárach*. Green Linnet Records.

——. 2010. *Ceol is Cuimhne (Music and Memory)*. Green Linnet Records.

——. 2013. *Ainneoin Na Stoirme (In Spite of the Storm)*. Green Linnet Records.

Uiscedwr. 2004. *Everywhere*. Yukka Records.

> Cormac Byrne provides innovative percussive accompaniment on drum kit, bodhrán, and bones couched in a British folk music context.

Wynne, John. 2000. *With Every Breath*. Cló Iar-Chonnacht.

> Seamus O'Kane accompanies Irish traditional music on bodhrán and bones.

Yates, Neil. 2011. *Five Countries*. Edition Records.

> In an acoustic jazz trio format, Cormac Byrne rhythmically accompanies on bodhrán, cajón, and cymbals.

DOCUMENTARIES: RADIO, FILM, AND TELEVISION

Ar Stáitse. 1976. "Dé Danann Live at the Embankment." Produced by TG4, Galway.

> This restored concert footage captures Dé Danann with Frankie Gavin, Alec Finn, Johnny Moynihan, and Johnny "Ringo" McDonagh on bodhrán.

Ar Thóir an Cheoil. 2013. "Beoga." Directed and produced by Méabh O'Hare, TG4, Galway.

> This series documenting upcoming Irish traditional groups features Eamon Murray on bodhrán with Beoga.

Beoga: Live at 10: The 10th Anniversary Concert. 2014. Produced by Compass Records, Nashville.

> This CD/DVD release features a full-length concert with Eamon Murray on bodhrán.

Blas Ceoil. 2009. Series 2, episode 4. Produced by BBC 2, Northern Ireland.

> This music program displays the Irish traditional music group Four Men and a Dog, featuring the bodhrán accompaniment of Gino Lupari.

——. 2009. Series 2, episode 5. Produced by BBC 2, Northern Ireland.

> The Boys of the Lough perform live with bodhrán accompaniment by Robin Morton.

——. 2010. Series 3, episode 1. Produced by BBC 2, Northern Ireland.

> Live concert footage of Flook is shown on this television series featuring the bodhrán accompaniment of John Joe Kelly.

Bosca Ceoil. 2014. Episode 5. Produced by TG4, Galway.

> This live music program features Cónal O'Grada and Colm Murphy (bodhrán), Alan Kelly and Jim Higgins (bodhrán), and Danú.

——. 2014. Episode 7. Produced by TG4, Galway.

> The trio of Luke Daniels, John Joe Kelly (bodhrán), and Ed Boyd perform live.

——. 2014. Episode 9. Produced by TG4, Galway.

This live music program features the trio of Joanie Madden, John Joe Kelly (bodhrán) and Seamie O'Dowd, and Four Men and a Dog featuring the bodhrán accompaniment of Gino Lupari.

——. 2014. Episode 10. Produced by TG4, Galway.

This live music program features the Alan Kelly Gang with Jim Higgins (bodhrán).

——. 2014. Episode 11. Produced by TG4, Galway.

The trio of Diarmaid Moynihan, Donncha Moynihan, and Eamon Murray (bodhrán) perform live.

——. 2014. Episode 12. Produced by TG4, Galway.

Beoga performs with Eamon Murray on bodhrán.

——. 2014. Episode 13. Produced by TG4, Galway.

Pauline Scanlon performs on stage with Flook featuring John Joe Kelly on bodhrán. Dervish also performs with Cathy Jordan on bodhrán.

Céilí House. 1955. Produced by Peter Browne, RTÉ Radio 1, Dublin.

Hosted by Kieran Hanrahan, this long-running radio show broadcasts local, acclaimed, traditional musicians from around Ireland in a session format.

Ceird an Cheoil. 2008. "Seamus O'Kane." Directed by Méabh O'Hare and written by Méabh O'Hare and Conor Byrne, TG4, Galway.

This documentary episode examines the place of the bodhrán in Irish music over the last fifty years, following bodhrán maker Seamus O'Kane through the different stages of his craft.

Celtic Connections. 2017. Episode 2: "Four Men and a Dog & Dónal O'Connor." TG4, Galway.

This music series features Four Men and a Dog with Gino Lupari on bodhrán.

Ceolchuairt. 2008. "Rónán & Rossa Ó Snodaigh in India." Produced by Magamedia, TG4, Galway.

Rossa and Rónán Ó Snodaigh of Kíla journey to Varanasi, India, on a musical pilgrimage that ends with a musical interaction with Zakir Hussain.

The Chieftains: An Irish Evening. 2000. Produced by BMG, Berlin.

The Chieftains perform Irish traditional music with a few musical guests such as Roger Daltrey, lead singer of the Who. This concert features Kevin Conneff on bodhrán.

The Chieftains: Down the Old Plank Road – The Nashville Sessions. 2003. Produced by Sony Legacy, New York City.

The Chieftains perform with country western and bluegrass musicians such as Alison Krauss, Earl Scruggs, and Emmylou Harris. Kevin Conneff is featured on bodhrán.

The Chieftains: Live at Montreux. 1997. Produced by Eagle Rock, London.

This live concert features Irish traditional music performed by the Chieftains with Kevin Conneff on bodhrán.

Christy Moore and Friends. 1980. Video recording. RTÉ Television, Dublin.
Christy Moore is joined by Planxty in live performance from the Abbey
Tavern in Howth, North County Dublin, featuring Moore's hand-striking
technique on the bodhrán.

*Come West along the Road: Irish Traditional Music — Treasures from RTE TV
Archives, 1960s–1980s.* 2007. RTÉ Television, Dublin.
This music series featured programs with different groupings of Irish
traditional musicians including performances by bodhrán players (e.g.,
Seamus Tansey, Seamus Donoghue) featuring varied tipper styles (e.g., hand,
double-ended tipper, and single-ended tipper playing).

Dambé: The Mali Project. 2008. Directed by Dearbhla Glynn and produced by
Vanessa Gildea, Irish Film Board, Galway.
Liam Ó Maonlaí (voice, bodhrán and harp) and Paddy Keenan (uilleann
pipes) interact with Malian musicians culminating in a performance at the
Festival au Désert.

Danú — One Night Stand. 2005. Produced by Shanachie Records, Newton, NJ.
This live performance features Donnchadh Gough on bodhrán.

Dervish: Live at Johnny Fox's. 1995. Produced by Video Music, Inc., Media, PA.
This live concert set in an Irish pub features Cathy Jordan on bodhrán.

Dervish: Midsummer's Night. 2005. Produced by Whirling Discs, Sligo.
Shot in Spiddal, Galway, this live performance displays Cathy Jordan's
bodhrán accompaniment.

Documentary on One. 2006. "Milltown Bodhrán Festival." Produced by Ronan
Kelly, RTÉ Radio 1, Dublin.
This radio documentary explores the ill-fated, bodhrán-centric music festival
that drew together an international group of competing and performing
percussionists.

———. 2016. "Peadar Mercier." Produced by Mel Mercier with Liam O'Brien,
RTÉ Radio 1, Dublin.
Mel Mercier explores the professional and personal life of his father, Peadar
Mercier, who was one of the influential bodhrán and bones players for the
Chieftains.

The Drum Maker. 2015. Directed and produced by Blayne Chastain, Bavaria.
A brief documentary that explores the drum making and life of German
bodhrán maker Christian Hedwitschak.

Fleadh TV. 2014. TG4, Galway.
This music program broadcasts live from the Fleadh Cheoil na hÉireann. Full
and edited video clips of top Irish traditional musicians including current
professional bodhrán performers are provided.

Geantraí. 1996. Television series. TG4, Galway.
This long-running television series features acclaimed Irish traditional
musicians in staged local pub sessions around Ireland. A slew of famous

bodhrán players ranging from Johnny McDonagh to Eamon Murray perform.

The Hands & Hearts of the Music Makers. 2017. Season 2, episode 1. Produced by Nuala Macklin, Newstalk Documentaries, Dublin.

Focusing upon the art of Irish traditional instrument making, Seamus O'Kane is interviewed about his long career as an influential bodhrán maker and performer.

Kíla: Live at Vicar St. 2002. Directed and produced by Kíla Records, Dublin.

This early documentary captures a live concert in the early days of Kíla with Rónán Ó Snodaigh on bodhrán.

Kíla: Once upon a Time. 2008. Directed by Neil Jordan, Traditions, Dublin.

This live concert documents *Kila* with Rónán Ó Snodaigh on bodhrán performing in Dublin.

Kíla: Pota Óir. 2017. Directed by Anthony White, White Washed Films, Dublin.

This documentary features extensive footage of Rónán Ó Snodaigh singing and performing on bodhrán.

Planxty: Live at Vicar Street. 2004. Directed by Tina Moran and Philip King. Produced by Philip King and Nuala O'Connor, Columbia Sony Music, New York City.

This reunion concert of Planxty features the hand-striking bodhrán accompaniment of Christy Moore and Dónal Lunny.

The Pure Drop. 1979. "Stocktons Wing: Dé Danann." Produced by RTÉ Television, Dublin.

This music program features a performance by Stockton's Wing with Tommy Hayes on bodhrán. A second performance by Dé Danann is included with bodhrán accompaniment by Johnny "Ringo" McDonagh.

Seán Ó Riada Memorial Concert. 1972. Produced by RTÉ Television, Dublin.

This live broadcast from the Gaiety Theatre shows members of Ceoltóirí Chualann, including Peadar Mercier on bodhrán.

Seán Ó Riada Second Memorial Concert. 1981. Produced by RTÉ Television, Dublin.

This second memorial concert was held in the Cork Opera House with musicians chosen by Paddy Glackin performing Ceoltóirí Chualann arrangements featuring Mel Mercier on bodhrán.

The Transatlantic Sessions Series 1. 1995. Programme 4. BBC Scotland, BBC 4, and RTÉ Television, Glasgow.

This episode provides a rare video example of Jim Sutherland's bodhrán playing with his homemade brush tipper. Sutherland also plays on a thick book with a large wooden tipper during the credits.

The Transatlantic Sessions Series 2. 1998. Programme 7. BBC Scotland, BBC 4, and RTÉ Television, Glasgow.

This episode offers a medley of Scottish *puirt à beul* (a form of lilting tunes) and Irish jigs as accompanied on bodhrán by Tommy Hayes.

LITERARY FICTION

Keane, John B. 1959. *Síve*. Dublin: Progress House.

Set in Listowel, Kerry, early productions featured Sonny Canavan's bodhráns, when one of the characters sings a song in the play and is accompanied on bodhrán.

——. 1986. *The Bodhrán Makers*. New York: Four Walls Eight Windows.

This humorous novel explores small-town sociocultural life and religion in Ireland featuring vivid descriptions of the wren boys ritual as well as the process for making a bodhrán.

Conclusion

As bodhrán players in Ireland and abroad are exposed to Irish and other music, they must navigate through this abundance of information and construct an aesthetic that represents their view of what constitutes Irish traditional music today. This is a process of cultural negotiation that addresses issues of assimilation, relocation, and the flow of information in musical communities. Since bodhrán players must mediate between different musical influences, it is useful to analyze the manner in which they do so.

This process has also altered bodhrán educational practices. Historically, since Irish traditional music is an aural tradition, musicians were expected to develop their playing through years of listening, practicing, and performing without the use of musical notation. However, established bodhrán players such as Belfast-born Steáfán Hannigan and Albany, New York, native Robert Daly have produced instructional texts and videos that use drum notation.

Daly applies snare drum exercises to the bodhrán. He uses a system in which European written notation is combined with arrows to indicate stick direction as well as colored and open circles to indicate hand placement. These snare patterns are used as exercises to apply to reel and jig patterns. The notation book also contains bodhrán drum patterns in unusual time signatures such as 7/8 and 5/4.

Hannigan also wrote a book that uses western notation with arrows to show tipper direction. He has since produced a video featuring demonstrations, playing techniques, western notation of reels and jigs, and a discussion of conceptual approaches. The DVD is accompanied by a detailed booklet describing musical forms such as the reel or jig as well as notated examples of specific rhythm patterns.

Daly cited Hannigan's notational system as needing further development. Having played the drum kit in country-western and rock bands, Daly sought to combine western percussion notation and the Irish aural tradition into a cohesive educational package that attempts to reconcile the different musical traditions. Rather than compartmentalize each musical experience into genre-based groups, Daly and Hannigan synthesized their experiences into a cohesive whole that was best transmitted through the creation of a new form of bodhrán instruction.

These developments not only exemplify on a micro level the influence and exchange between Ireland and Irish diasporic communities but also represent a step toward increasing the speed with which musicians can learn the bodhrán. In 2008 Daly mentioned in an interview that his primary reason for learning and performing Irish traditional music was to reconnect with his Irish heritage.

In an interview with Cathy Clarke, an amateur bodhrán player also living in Albany, she mentioned that she learned to play through the aural tradition. She relied on learning from recordings of great bodhrán players such as Johnny McDonagh, Colm Murphy, and Tommy Hayes. These recordings replaced the tradition of performing in sessions and afforded Clarke the opportunity to practice at home. It was years later that she finally began playing in local sessions.

Like Daly, Clarke emphasized that she hoped to reconnect with and deepen her understanding of her own Irish heritage. She had never visited Ireland, and so her performance of Irish traditional music served as her means of imagining Ireland and fostering her own relationship to perceived Irishness. When performing in Albany sessions, Clarke found that many of the musicians were also connecting to their Irish heritage.

Dermot Sheedy, a bodhrán player based in Limerick, viewed his performances as the continuation of a tradition that had been aurally passed down from one generation of Irish musicians to another. His method of learning was based on the aural tradition, although he practiced with recordings. His sense of cultural inheritance and ownership differed from Daly and Clarke's concept of Irishness in that it did not represent something that had been lost and needed to be rediscovered. Instead, it was the continuation of an unbroken organic tradition that he was connecting to through musical performance. However, Sheedy's engagement with traditional music still involved imagining an Irish tradition that incorporated the bodhrán well before the 1950s. Sheedy's connection with past generations was imagined and intensified through continual performance.

Eamon Murray of Beoga further supported the aural learning method.

For the students I have regularly, I have them watch and learn. I don't really use any specific notation. I like to bounce off the students and have them bounce off me. I try to get them to groove instead of just playing up and down. I give them a basic skill set and then have them accompany music in the way they want to and the way I tell them. My session playing is very different from when I perform, and what I perform is very different from what I teach. I try to encourage my students to sit in the pocket. Never to try too much to do the perfect thing for the music. A lot of times the students will bring me things they like or a tune from a session or preparing for a fleadh. It should be a lot more musical than a lot of people make it.

Murray's pedagogical stance resonates with the older method of learning. Given the pluralistic approach to teaching the bodhrán, it is no surprise that teachers and students are drawing upon resources from various percussion traditions to supplement their musical practice. In an effort to further the instrument's application, technique, and pedagogy, leading practitioners have drawn inspiration from eclectic sources, indicating an ongoing period of exploration that questions time-honored musical practices.

Emphasizing a hybrid approach to bodhrán pedagogy, Martin O'Neill told me:

When I teach now, my methods are a lot more disciplined than when I was taught growing up. The bodhrán has progressed at such a fast rate that the knowledge and the skills are completely different than they were twenty years ago or more. I would try to enforce discipline in terms of rudiments and techniques, as well as using your ears and getting a feel for the music. Try to marry the aural tradition with the more developed technical aspect of it. Anything that involved a paradiddle, those type of rudiments that involve single strokes and a set of double strokes would be used as exercises or in my playing. I don't directly translate double down and double up. Or up down up. I don't see any advantage to it. Don't always connect left with down and right with up. I would use a lot of snare techniques. I have dipped into some classical snare repertoire that would specifically use alternate strokes and apply them to the bodhrán for developing technique, because there is such a wealth of stuff already written that whether it is orchestral snare or marching snare, it seems a waste not to. The way I see the bodhránor use it in a contemporary traditional environment, I don't have this pigeonhole idea of the bodhrán only playing Irish music or Scottish music or traditional music, so I don't see any problem with moving it away and using different repertoire or other influences. For me, it is a drum that works in so many different environments.

Mirroring this inclusive pedagogical approach, Cormac Byrne said, "For bodhrán players, I encourage them to study other percussion and to be able to write it. If you can't sing it, you can't play it, and if you can't write it, you can't play it. If you can visualize it and figure out where everything should sit, it makes things easier."

In an effort to broaden the musical application and role of the bodhrán, select performers and educators such as O'Neill and Byrne are keen to exploit resources that can facilitate the inclusion of the bodhrán into a larger cosmopolitan percussion narrative. Through the embrace of various percussion traditions, the aforementioned bodhrán players are seeking to integrate the bodhrán into the wider canon of world percussion traditions, thus providing performers with opportunities outside the confines of Irish traditional music.

As a music teacher in a public high school in Bronx, New York, I was intrigued by the bodhrán's initial simplicity of sound production, musical versatility (genres, timbres, techniques, and accompaniment), size, portability, dynamic and register range (bass to treble), and instrumental commonalities with other frame drum musical traditions found around the world. Due to the adaptability of the instrument to different musical contexts, the bodhrán appeared to be a wonderful solution to classroom percussive music making.

Leading an Afro-Latin percussion ensemble at Kappa High School, I began incorporating the bodhrán into class rehearsals when we performed West African and Afro-Latin music, particularly Yoruba Bembe, Kuku (Guinea-Bissau), and mambo. The introduction of a new percussion instrument into ensemble rehearsals allowed for greater experimentation. As part of our rehearsals of West African Bembe in 12/8 meter, I asked students to transition to frame drums. Students were grouped according to their four parts: cowbell pattern, hand drum pattern, bass drum pattern, and the shaker pattern. Students were required to find tippers suitable for executing their parts. Students were then asked to map the patterns on the drums in order to find a pleasing or similar sounding part to the one executed on the hand drums, cowbell, shakers, and bass drums. Through group discussion, they decided that the wire brush tipper would play the shaker part. The wooden tippers hit against the hard wooden frame would play the cowbell part. The wooden tippers with drum skin hand muting would play the hand drum pattern requiring a difficult up-up-down, down-up-up sticking pattern. The felt tippers were chosen to play the bass drum pattern. I performed with the students, vocalizing their parts to facilitate greater musical cohesion.

West African Bembe and Cuban mambo were mapped, orchestrated, and performed on the bodhráns through an experimental process. By trial and error, students were able to take greater ownership for their respective parts as they devised how to execute the percussion music. Given that these musical forms are not traditionally played on the bodhrán, the students had fewer limitations and cultural expectations for how the parts should sound or be played. In addition, students discovered techniques for executing their musical parts, ranging from different sticking patterns, skin muting, individual polyrhythmic drumming, hand techniques, pitch slides, and tippers. Students also explored bodhrán group percussion arrangements, which departs from many frame drum accompaniment traditions. The opportunity to experiment with this versatile drum fostered greater student expression, ownership, and engagement.

By changing the format and role of the bodhrán from a single accompanying percussion instrument to a percussion ensemble, the instrument was reconceptualized as a world percussion instrument that could be included in a variety of musical contexts and performance roles, ranging from soloist to polyrhythmic percussion group performer. The musical versatility of this instrument and its possibility as an educational tool have yet to be fully realized on stage or in the classroom.

FUTURE OF THE BODHRÁN

As evidenced by the evolving nature of bodhrán construction, performance practices, and pedagogy, the future of the bodhrán remains uncertain. The many possible uses for the instrument suggest a varied cosmopolitan existence. Bodhrán maker Rob Forkner explains:

> The music has gone toward new traditional fusion, gaining a wider audience and different sets of expectations that come with the drum. Drums have to be made to allow certain sounds to happen much more efficiently. In the late 1980s, I learned the tunes first and the drum was an accompany instrument. You wouldn't learn it like a drum but more like a bass guitar. That has changed a lot. Nowadays you have teaching that has to do with patterns and rhythmic traditional drumming styles. The bodhrán is evolving out of the sessions into new traditional/jazz settings and even beyond, where the drum is a more rhythmic instrument or sometimes lead instrument. As a result, a lot of drum makers now are behind players who are suited and tailored for these sounds. It is almost a different instrument.

Cormac Byrne further expounded on Forkner's observation, stating that current bodhrán players need a world music perspective in order to choose the best approach for learning and playing the drum. Byrne felt that adapting world percussion traditions to the bodhrán was more engaging and artistically satisfying when compared with the perceived strictures of Irish traditional bodhrán accompaniment. Eamon Murray echoed this sentiment, explaining that he hoped bodhrán accompaniment would eventually reach a similar status and level of musical complexity as tabla accompaniment in Indian classical music. He lamented the fact that Irish traditional musicians had fully exhausted the possibilities of playing in 4/4 and 6/8 meter.

Martin O'Neill elaborated:

> Bodhrán construction is constantly being refined. When I started playing the bodhrán, I couldn't have imagined I would be able to do the things I can do now. It just wasn't possible on the drums I was playing. The first time I got to play a Seamus O'Kane drum I was just blown away. The possibilities that opened up seemed limitless compared with the drum I was playing at the time. Never in a million years would I be able to replicate any of these sounds, and all of a sudden I had so much range and variety of tone and timbre. Hedwitschak's drum I am playing with now allows me to express myself in the way I want to do that. The tuning holds, I haven't been let down by the drum, I can push it and it will respond to that, and it will keep up with what I am trying to do. The only thing I can hope for is that as the development of the drum continues, it will inspire me to try new things.

Both bodhrán makers and players envision a near future in which instrumental growth and experimentation continue onward. The possibilities for further refinement of drum construction and the inclusion of the drum in music of the world suggest a hopeful, relevant future. While historically rooted in Irish culture, the drum is advancing beyond the boundaries of Irish traditional music into the unchartered depths of musics of the world through participation, performance, and instrument making.

Bibliography

Anderson, Benedict. 1983. *Imagined Communities: Reflections on the Origin and Spread of Nationalism*. London: Verso.

Beck, Ulrich, Scott Lash, and Anthony Giddens. 1994. *Reflexive Modernization: Politics, Tradition, and Aesthetics in the Modern Social Order*. Palo Alto: Stanford University Press.

Bijker, Wiebe E., and Thomas P. Hughes and Trevor J. Pinch (ed.) (1987) *The Social Construction of Technological Systems: New Directions in the Sociology and History of Technology*, Cambridge: MIT Press.

Bodhran DVD, The. 2005. Video recording. London: Music Sales.

Breathnach, Breandan. 1996. *Folk Music and Dances of Ireland*. Cork: Mercier Press.

Buchanan, Donna A. 1995. "Metaphors of Power, Metaphors of Truth: The Politics of Music Professionalism in Bulgarian Folk Orchestras." *Ethnomusicology* 39 (3): 381–416.

Carson, Ciaran. 1986. *Pocket Guide to Irish Traditional Music*. Belfast: Appletree Press.

Cooper, David. 2009. *The Musical Traditions of Northern Ireland and Its Diaspora: Community and Conflict*. London: Ashgate.

Daly, Robert. 2007. *The Bodhrán: An Irish Drum*. Albany: Celtic Percussion.

Dickinson, Peter, ed. 2006. *Cage Talk: Dialogues with and about John Cage*. Rochester: University of Rochester Press.

Dineen, Patrick S. 1904. *Foclóir Gaedhilge agus Béarla: An Irish-English Dictionary*. Dublin: M. H. Gill for the Irish Text Society.

Duffy, Paddy. "The Wren." *Ashbourne Wren Boys*. Tumblr. Web. Accessed May 7, 2015.

Feld, Steven. 1984. "Communication, Music, and Speech about Music." *Yearbook for Traditional Music* 16: 1–18.

Fleming, Rachel. 2004. "Resisting Cultural Standardization: Comhaltas Ceoltóirí Éireann and the Revitalization of Traditional Music in Ireland." *Journal of Folklore Research* 41 (2/3): Special Double Issue: Advocacy Issues in Folklore, 227–57.

Forkner, Rob. "Drums." *Metloef Irish Drums*. Web. Accessed May 14, 2015.

Forsthoff, K., and Andy Kruspe. 2013. "The Irish Bodhrán in Context: Celebrating the Evolutions of a Modern Tradition." *Percussive Notes* 51 (5): 20–22.

Glatt, John. 1997. *The Chieftains: An Authorized Biography*. London: St. Martin's Press.

Green, Lucy. 2001. *How Popular Musicians Learn: A Way Ahead for Music Education*. London: Ashgate Press.

———. 2008. *Music, Informal Learning, and the School: A New Classroom Pedagogy*. London: Ashgate Press.

Hannigan, Steáfán. 1991. *The Bodhrán Book*. Cork: Ossian.

Hedwitschak, Christian. "Bodhráns' Hedwitschak Drums: Art Bodhrán." Web. Accessed May 14, 2015.

Higgins, Jim. 2005. *Forms, Approaches, and Timbre Production in the Contemporary Bodhrán*. Limerick: University of Limerick.

Inda, Jonathan Xavier, and Renato Rosaldo, eds. 2002. *The Anthropology of Globalization: A Reader*. Oxford: Blackwell.

Keane, John B. 1959. *Sive*. Dublin: Progress House.

———. 1992. *The Bodhrán Makers*. New York: Four Walls Eight Windows.

Kearney, Daithí. 2013. "Regions, Regionality, and Regionalization in Irish Traditional Music: The Role of *Comhaltas Ceoltóirí Éireann*." *Ethnomusicology Ireland* 2 (3): 72–94.

Kearns, Malachy. 1996. *Wallup: Humour and Lore of Bodhrán Making*. Connemara: Roundstone Music Instruments.

Klein, Hans K. and Daniel Lee Kleinman (2002) 'The Social Construction of Technology: Structural Considerations', Science, Technology, & Human Values, 27, 1, (Winter), 28–52.

Lysaght, Patricia (2002) 'Kevin Danaher (Caoimhin O Danachair), 1913–2002. (in Memoriam)', *Folklore*, 113, 2, 261–264.

Mack, Ariel, ed. 1997. *Technology and the Rest of Culture*. Columbus: Ohio State University Press.

Mallinson, Dave, ed. 2007. *The Irish Drum, An Bodhrán: A Tutor by Peter Houlihan*. West Yorkshire: A Mally Production.

Marshall, Mark, Matthias Rath, and Breege Moynihan. 2002. "The Virtual Bodhrán: The Vodhran." *Proceedings of the 2002 Conference on New Instruments for Musical Expression (NIME-02)*, 1–2. Dublin.

Mazzarella, William. 2004. "Culture, Globalization, Mediation." *Annual Review of Anthropology* 33 (1): 345–67.

Mc Cionnaith, Láimhbheartach. 1935. *Foclóir Béarla agus Gaedhilge: English-Irish Dictionary*. Dublin: Oifig Díolta Foillseacháin Rialtais.

McCrickard, Janet E. 1987. *The Bodhrán: The Background to the Traditional Irish Drum*. Glastonbury: Fieldfare Art and Design.

Monson, Ingrid. 1999. "Riffs, Repetition, and Theories of Globalization." *Ethnomusicology* 43 (1): 31–65.

Morrison, Scott. 2011. "The History of the Bodhrán: Ireland's 'Native Drum.'" *Percussive Notes* 49 (3): 38–41.

Motherway, Susan H. 2013. *The Globalization of Irish Traditional Song Performance*. Burlington, VT: Ashgate.

Ó Bharáin, Liam. 2007. "Bodhrán – Its Origin, Meaning, and History." *Treoir* 39 (4): 50–56.

———. 2008a. "Bodhrán – Its Recent History: Making and Playing the Bodhrán." *Treoir* 40 (1): 47–52.

———. 2008b. "Bodhrán – Its Recent History: Making and Playing the Bodhrán." *Treoir* 40 (2): 49–56.

Ó hAllmhuráin, Gearóid. 1998. *A Pocket History of Irish Traditional Music*. Dublin: O'Brien Press.

Ó Súilleabháin, Mícheál. 1974. "The Bodhrán." *Treoir* 6: 4–5.

———. 1984. *The Bodhrán: An Easy to Learn Method for the Complete Beginner Showing the Different Regional Styles and Techniques*. Waltons Irish Music.

Ógáin, Ríonach uí. 2002. "'A Tune off the River': The Lore of Musical Instruments in the Irish Tradition." *Béaloideas* 70: 127–52.

———, ed. 2009. *Going to the Well for Water: The Séamus Ennis Field Diary, 1942–1946*. Cork: Cork University Press.

O'Kane, Seamus. "Tensioning." *Seamus O'Kane*. Trad Centre. Web. Accessed May 14, 2015.

O'Mahoney, Terry. 1999. "The Irish Bodhrán." *Percussive Notes* 7 (2): 34–40.

O'Meara, John J. 1982. *Gerald of Wales: The History and Topography of Ireland*. Rev. ed. Harmondsworth: Penguin.

Penley, Constance, and Andrew Ross, eds. 1991. *Technoculture*. Minneapolis: University of Minnesota Press.

Schiller, Rina. 2001. *The Lambeg and the Bodhrán*. Belfast: Queen's University.

Settles, David. Catalog. *Davey Drums*. Web. Accessed May 14, 2015.

Stokes, Martin, ed. 1994. *Ethnicity, Identity, and Music: The Musical Construction of Place*. Oxford: Berg.

Stokes, Martin, and Philip V. Bohlman, eds. 2003. *Celtic Modern: Music at the Global Fringe*. Oxford: Scarecrow Press.

Such, David G. 1985. "The Bodhrán: The Black Sheep in the Family of Traditional Irish Musical Instruments." *Galpin Society Journal* 38: 9–19.

Taylor, Timothy. 2001. *Strange Sounds: Music, Technology & Culture*. New York: Routledge.

Turino, Thomas. 2000. *Nationalists, Cosmopolitans, and Popular Music in Zimbabwe*, Chicago: University of Chicago Press.

Vallely, Fintan, ed. 1999. *The Companion to Irish Traditional Music*. Cork: Cork University Press.

Wagels, Rolf. "The History." *Craiceann*. Newsletter. Web. Accessed May 19, 2015.

Westrum, Ron. 1991. *Technologies & Society: The Shaping of People and Things*. Belmont: Wadsworth.

Williams, Sean, and Lillis Ó Laoire. 2011. *Bright Star of the West: Joe Heaney, Irish Song Man*. Oxford: Oxford University Press.

INTERVIEWS WITH AUTHOR

Bartlett, Darius. April 7, 2015.
Blackwell, John. April 21, 2015.
Broeck, Jef van Den. April 4, 2015.
Byrne, Cormac. April 9, 2015.
Clancy, Paddy. July 26, 2015.
Clarke, Cathy. January 12, 2008.
Cooperman, Patrick. March 3, 2015.
Coughlan, Owen. April 3, 2008.
Cuyler, Brent. May 26, 2015.
Daly, Robert. January 14, 2008.
Davenport, Josie. April 5, 2015.
Davey, Junior. April 14, 2015.
Davey, Sonny. June 4, 2015.
Di Blasi, Joan. May 29, 2015.
Falconer, Gordon. June 3, 2015.
Forkner, Robert. April 7, 2015.
Forman, Steve. July 14, 2015.
Griffin, Mossie. May 14, 2015.
Hall, Barry. June 1, 2015.
Hannigan, Steáfán. April 2, 2015.
Hayes, Tommy. April 13, 2015.
Hedwitschak, Christian. April 2, 2015.
Hernon, Mai Dodd. June 2, 2015.
Higgins, Jim. March 20, 2015.
Joyce, Sandra. March 12, 2008.
Lee, Paul Fraser. May 31, 2015.
March, Ben. April 8, 2015.
Mercier, Mel. March 5, 2008.
Moore, Christy. June 3, 2015.
Morton, Robin. May 20, 2015.
Motooka, Toshia. April 2, 2015.
Munnelly, Kieran. April 2, 2015.
Murray, Eamon. April 3, 2015.
Ó Snodaigh, Rónán. April 6, 2015.
O'Kane, Seamus. April 8, 2015.
O'Neill, Martin. April 8, 2015.
Pazer, Jonathan. May 29, 2015.

Phelan, Colm. April 6, 2015.

Prieto, Martín Domínguez. April 10, 2015.

Quinlan, Mike. May 26, 2015.

Ranney, Joanne. October 16, 2015.

Reilly, Ozzie. April 14, 2015.

Ryan, Barbara. May 14, 2015.

Settles, David. April 1, 2015.

Sheedy, Dermot. March 7, 2008.

Sutherland, Jim. May 27, 2015.

Tansey, Seamus. May 29 and 31, 2015.

Wagels, Dr. Rolf. April 3, 2015.

Walsh, Robbie. May 26, 2015.

White, Brendan. April 7, 2015.

DISCOGRAPHY

Cooley, Joe. 1975. *Cooley*. Gael-Linn.

Davey, Junior. 2005. *A Sound Skin*. Coleman Heritage Center.

Hayes, Tommy. 1995. *An Rás*. Mulligan.

McGowan, Ted. 1999. *The Mountain Road: A Compilation of Tunes Popular in South Sligo*. Coleman Heritage Center.

Morrison, Tom, and John Reynolds. 1927. *Columbia 33210-F*. 78 rpm.

———. 1927. *Columbia 33247-F*. 78 rpm.

———. 1927. *Columbia 33260-F*. 78 rpm.

———. 1927. *Columbia 33308-F*. 78 rpm.

———. 1928. *Columbia 33293-F*. 78 rpm.

Murphy, Colm. 1996. *An Bodhrán*. Gael-Linn.

Planxty. 1973a. *Planxty*. Shanachie. CD.

———. 1973b. *Well Below the Valley*. Shanachie.

———. 1974. *Cold Blow and the Rainy Night*. Shanachie.

———. 1979. *After the Break*. Shanachie Records.

———. 1980. *The Woman I Loved So Well*. Tara Music.

———. 1983. *Words & Music*. Shanachie.

Stockton's Wing. 1978. *Stockton's Wing*. Tara Music.

Index

About the Author

Photo courtesy of Robert Presciutti, January 2020.

Colin Harte teaches ethnomusicology in the City University of New York Irish Studies department and leads an Afro-Latin percussion ensemble for the New York City Department of Education. His articles and reviews have appeared in *Ethnomusicology Forum*, *Smithsonian Folkways*, *New Hibernia Review*, *Folk Music Journal*, and the *Bardian*, among other publications. A pianist and bodhrán percussionist, he founded the University of Florida Irish Traditional Music Ensemble and plays in New York's Brazilian, jazz, and Irish communities.